STUDIES IN ROMANCE LANGUAGES: 22

THE PERILOUS HUNT

Symbols in Hispanic
and European Balladry

Edith Randam Rogers

THE UNIVERSITY PRESS OF KENTUCKY

Library of Congress Cataloging in Publication Data

Rogers, Edith Randam, 1924-
    The perilous hunt.

    (Studies in Romance languages; 22)
    Bibliography: p.
    Includes indexes.
    1. Ballads, European—History and criticism.
    2. Ballads, Spanish—History and criticism.
    3. Symbolism in literature.   4. Literature, Com-
    parative—Themes, motives.   I. Title.   II. Series.
    PN1376.R6   809.1'4   79-4010
    ISBN 0-8131-1396-2

Scholarly publisher for the Commonwealth,
serving Berea College, Centre College of Kentucky,
Eastern Kentucky University, The Filson Club,
Georgetown College, Kentucky Historical Society,
Kentucky State University, Morehead State University,
Murray State University, Northern Kentucky University,
Transylvania University, University of Kentucky,
University of Louisville, and Western Kentucky University.

Editorial and Sales Offices: Lexington, Kentucky 40506

To Helle

CONTENTS

PREFACE

This book highlights a small number of symbols that may occur in a large number of ballads, and the interpretations are intended to be applicable not only to the ballads analyzed here but to many others that are not mentioned. Therefore, the list of examples is selective rather than exhaustive. So as to keep the book from growing to unmanageable size, only occasional comparisons are made outside the genre and no interpretations are attempted on the basis of, for instance, psychoanalysis or the study of myth, even though such approaches look highly promising. Regrettably, but unavoidably, many ballads had to be used in translation, with all the usual drawbacks. Some valuable reference works, such as the *Romancero tradicional de las lenguas hispánicas, Deutsche Volkslieder mit ihren Melodien,* or S. G. Armistead's and J. H. Silverman's *Judeo-Spanish Chapbooks,* could not be fully utilized, either because they are still in the process of publication or because they appeared after the basic research for the present study had been completed.

Six journals have kindly permitted the use of material from my previously published articles: "El Conde Olinos: Metempsychosis or Miracle," *Bulletin of Hispanic Studies* 50 (1973):325-39; "Games of Muscle, Mind, and Chance," *Hispania* 55 (1972):419-27; "The Hunt in the *Romancero* and Other Traditional Ballads," *Hispanic Review* 42 (1974):133-71; "Magic Music: A Self-Centered Ballad Motif," *Kentucky Romance Quarterly* 22 (1975):263-92; "The Moral Standing of the Unkempt," *Southern Folklore Quarterly* 36 (1972):144-59; and "Clothing as a Multifarious Ballad Symbol," *Western Folklore* 34 (1975):261-97 (published by the California Folklore Society). I acknowledge gratefully the valuable advice of don Julio Caro Baroja, doña Pilar García de Diego, and Professor Felix Oinas, as well as the support of the Council of Research and Creative Work of the University of Colorado in preparing the manuscript and of the Committee on University Scholarly Publications of the University of Colorado in publishing the study.

1
INTRODUCTION

The undeniably healthy revolution in the study of folklore, with its mandate of scientific objectivity, has had an unfortunate (and doubtless unintended) by-product: the neglect of the traditional ballad as a form of art. The withdrawal of the literary critic from this field is partly due to the not entirely baseless charge that he has discriminated against aesthetically inferior texts.[1] Particularly in the last century, collectors, editors, and translators exercised their critical function somewhat high-handedly, by grading ballads as either "pretty" or "worthless" and by now improving, now discarding the versions that did not meet their artistic standards. The understandably negative reaction to such arbitrary management appears to have implicated all criticism that deals with ballads as imaginative literature and has led ballad scholars, including those who might otherwise employ an interpretation of the patterns of interwoven images and symbols, to concentrate on the tracing of the evolution and derivation of themes and motifs, often in conjunction with the publishing of previously inaccessible versions.

That the study of imagery in folk ballads has been leading a subterraneous life and is ready to emerge to a legitimate existence has become increasingly evident in certain recent publications, which, besides presenting newly discovered versions and proposing genealogies, probe also into the meaning and function of some of the component parts. At the same time, in the structure of those studies a particular ballad, rather than a motif, is the main unit.

Besides the self-explanatory precedence of the publishing of primary sources on the one hand and the taunt of excessive value judgment on the other, an additional cause of the paucity of analyses of poetic expression may have lain in the preemptive classification of the ballad as a narrative genre. In most ballads the more conspicuous element is indeed the narrative; the poetic aspect, therefore, has been given short shrift even in those cases where it deserves priority. Despite the narrative label, ballads have a way of usurping the tools of the lyric. Deceived by the seeming simplicity of style, we may fail to give due credit to the subtle means of implying, suggesting, or insinuating; but thinking back on a ballad we have heard, we find that somehow we know much more than we were told in words. We are aware, for example, of the intentions, expectations, emotions, sufferings, strengths, or failings of a girl. Or again, we know, long before the narrative reaches that point, whether the hero is going to triumph or to die. Should we now have the ballad repeated, we are likely to find that the explicit information in the text is about the girl's dress or the man's dogs, and that there is no mention of the girl's mood or the man's imminent fate.

My point is that the verse about the dress or the dogs is precisely what made us aware of all the things unsaid. That the imagery and the tropological aspect of ballad language are so often passed over is due to the fact that the symbols are apt to retain also their denotative, obvious, meaning. The girl's dress and the man's dogs are a rightful part of the story. In other words, the literal meaning of the image is not displaced by, but coexists with, its figurative meaning. This, while not the exclusive property of the poetic diction of ballads, is one of its essential characteristics. Although metaphors were standard language in artistic poetry and Petrarch's conceits were avidly reproduced and multiplied during the same centuries when in many countries popular ballads were evolving, the latter remained remarkably immune to those devices. Even when an allegory such as the love-hunt (discussed in chap. 2) happened to intrude in popular balladry, it soon tended to be taken literally.

This "real" quality of symbols is closely related to the eminently visual nature of ballad diction. Occidental culture, as it is, tends to communicate through the eyes; ballads, however, go even beyond the customary proportions in translating into visual terms many phenomena normally associated with any of the other four senses, or none of them. For instance, music becomes visual through the description of its effect: we see, rather than hear, birds stopping in their flight, fish rising to the surface of the sea, and doors opening by themselves. The pleasure of touch is communicated in visual terms when we watch a girl comb her lover's hair. We shall further see that various psychological processes also become visible. Joy and sorrow are shown by color and fabric of dress. Love may be expressed by combing the loved one's hair and by wearing or giving fine clothes. Waiting is shown by combing; agitation, by hasty dressing. Determination may be observed in British women as they gather up their clothes for efficient action; in Spanish men, as they abstain from combing and other similar comforts before a difficult enterprise; in women who wish to break down a man's will, as they choose a certain type of attire; in men who challenge fate, as they fling down dice or a game-board. Despair is demonstrated by dropping a comb or abandoning costly dress; a conflict between two wills, by a contest in a game. When a visual image is elaborated into a lengthy passage, it not only identifies but strengthens and prolongs the impact of an emotion: the vows of austerity occupying a goodly number of lines show either the force of determination or the depth and indelibility of sorrow. Even the subtle process of falling in love is put before the audience's eyes by means of an account of a table game or a description of the effects of music. The consistent translation of the narrative into visual imagery and the resulting limitation of the number of symbols lie at the root of the international character of the poetic expression in popular ballads. The singers have denied themselves a great deal of idiomatic elaboration of their respective languages in which a learned poet would feel free to indulge. Because of the—apparently obligatory—visual representation, the difference between comprehension of another nation's erudite poetry and an understanding of its popular balladry may be compared to the difference between comprehending a conventional alphabet and understanding pictograms.

Granted that an image may have different shades of meaning in different countries—a Spanish wife's dishabille usually suggests that she is expecting a lover, while a Russian wife is understood to be harboring one if she comes to the door in stocking feet—generally, a similar symbol carries a similar meaning. At the first reading of La Villemarqué's *Barzaz-Breiz*, I was impressed by the anomalous function of some motifs in Breton ballads, only to find later that nearly all of these particular ballads were listed as counterfeit in Luzel's exposé. Thus the language of ballads, paradoxically, rises above linguistic differences mainly because it does not depend so much on words as on the concreteness of the visual images created by words. The associations evoked by the symbols are sensory rather than conceptual or intellectual. Although a ballad employs words, its communication is largely nonverbal. Hence, it travels well.

The universality of ballad diction has been noted before, however. What does promise additional discoveries is the diversity within the universality, as the study of one body of ballads helps us understand another. Spanish *romances,* Danish *viser,* Breton *gwerziou,* Russian *byliny,* and the rest, may all be referred to as "ballads" for the sake of simplicity, but they are not the same. Some of the well-known characteristics of traditional *romances* are brevity, concision, ellipsis, and a strong lyric component. Consequently, we may be at a loss trying to explain some disconnected lines or those that seem to contribute only ornamental details. Should we, now, find a corresponding motif in a longer, more coherent ballad of another country, new light would be thrown on the Spanish song. A case in point is the motif of the dismal hunt, often dismissed as a commonplace in the *Romancero.* After we note in British ballads the significance of hawk and hound, in Slavic songs the personification of hunting birds, and in Scandinavian *viser* the uncanny creatures that inhabit the woods, the Spanish hunt reveals its reason of existence. Conversely, the tightness of form in the *Romancero,* which orders antithetical lines, such as those about contrasting clothes, into conspicuous blocks, calls attention to the function of similar antitheses dispersed over a long Scottish ballad. Since each country has retained or elaborated a different segment of a motif that at some remote hypothetical point in time was probably complete and clear, it is often very fruitful to reassemble such skewed local motifs in order to ascertain their meaning and function in obscure cases. While the focus of the present study is on the *Romancero,* ballads from at least a score of different European languages are included, so as to produce a meaningful contexture. Likewise, the very nature of the traditional ballad requires the examination of recently collected texts alongside those of authenticated age, as the Spanish *Primavera* series[2] or the Danish *viser.* Even within the *Romancero viejo,* there is some heterogeneity: uncontestably traditional songs alternate with occasional minstrel ballads and recastings by learned poets.[3] Barring from the discussion all dubious texts would unnecessarily impoverish the pool of resources. Not only are the borderlines between the categories hazy, but many motifs have passed from one category to another. Vertical mobility was characteristic of the *Romancero* during its period of bloom, which means that the motifs were the property of several classes of the population that differed from each other socially and intellectually.

At the same time, identity of meaning of a motif or symbol in different countries, different ages, or different classes, must not be accepted as a foregone conclusion. Only if the meaning truly fits the context should it be extended from one ballad to another. The context is, in fact, my principal basis for testing and determining the symbolism and function. While the sanctioned method for comparative studies—to seek, often in classical mythology, the oldest version and the origins of a theme or a motif—has led to a great deal of valuable knowledge, it does not always correctly identify the meaning within a given period or a particular social class. Just as Vergil is reincarnated in the *Romancero* as a ladies' man, many other characters and motifs have taken on new roles.

One might say that the popular ballad, by definition, should require no scholarly deciphering of its imagery in order to be understood. Ideally we get the message without being conscious of the mechanics, since it is communicated by an open code—open, that is, to anyone not severed from the deep roots of popular culture. To those endowed with native sensitivity to the symbolism of traditional ballads, I expect this study to offer less help in comprehending any particular text than in honing awareness of the means by which the ballad is so easily understood. The question to ask, then, is not "What does it say?" but "How did I know?"

2

ARCADIA AND APOCALYPSE
The Hunt

To say that hunting plays an important part in traditional ballads is both right and wrong. Hunters abound but seldom bring home any game; in the *Romancero,* the game is not even likely to appear. The reason for this lies in one of the main characteristics of balladry. Ballads deal with people and their relations with other people, or sometimes other anthropomorphic beings. Hunting is thus not the subject, but the scene, the circumstance, the atmosphere.

This does not mean that hunting skill failed to enhance the image of a medieval knight, as he appears in ballads. In the eulogy of the *Infantes de Salas (Prim.* 24), the distinction of two of the slain sons is proficiency in hunting:

> —Hijo Suero Gustos,   todo el mundo os estimaba;
> el rey os tuviera en mucho,   sólo para la su caza:
> gran caballero esforzado,   muy buen bracero a ventaja.
> . . . .
> —Oh hijo Fernán González,   nombre del mejor de España,
> . . . .
> matador de puerco espín,   amigo de gran compaña.

More often, however, not the accomplishment but the habit of hunting is mentioned, and the emphasis shifts, thus, from the quality of a hero to the quality of life. The Christian girl in *Don Bueso y su hermana,* riding with the young man who has rescued her from Moorish captivity, recognizes the countryside where her father and brother used to hunt:

> —Lloro porque en estos campos   mi padre a cazar venía,
> con mi hermano Moralejo   y toda su cortesía.[1]

What the girl remembers after her suffering in servitude is a stable, idyllic existence, for which the brother's hunting is one of several possible symbols, replaced in other, particularly the six-syllable, versions by different pastimes: "las cañas corría" or "los toros corría."[2] Peace of mind and hunting are connected in a more obvious way in the advice given in two Danish ballads to young knights who need to forget an impossible love:

> "Go then, and hunt the hart and hind;
> So banish Christel from thy mind.
>
> "Go, hunt the stag, go hunt the roe,
> And every thought of love forego."[3]

At times, though, the two-faced symbol shows its sinister side: peace of mind has hardened into callousness in *Lord Thomas and Lady Margaret* (Child 260), where, in a seemingly arcadian setting, the hunter turns his servants on his lady:

> Lord Thomas is to the hunting gone
> To hunt the fallow deer;
> Lady Margaret's to the greenwood shaw,
> To see her lover hunt there.[4]

For a king, the chase is an occasion to meet people of other walks of life, as in the humorous *King Edward the Fourth and a Tanner of Tamworth* (Child 273), or to talk to his courtiers, as in the tragic *Conde de Luna*, where he sends his noble hunting companion to death:

> El rey don Juan el segundo   dijo un día andando a caza
> al infante don Fadrique   que conde de Luna se llama,
> que a don García Fernández   le fuesse a ver a la cama.[5]

Menéndez y Pelayo (12:162) points out that, even in this detail, the *romance* follows closely the *Crónica de D. Juan II* of 1434.

While game receives only sporadic mention, "the insignia of a gentleman from Norway to Spain," both in fact and in song, are his hawk and hound—frequently included in portraits and tombstone effigies of illustrious persons. Documents tell of privileged nobles taking their falcons to Mass and even perching them on the edge of the altar.[6] More than mere complements, hawk and hound appear to be integral parts of a knight. Severe punishment consisted of blinding, and of cutting off the foot used for mounting a horse and the hand that held the hawk:

> Sácanle ambos los ojos,   los ojos de la su faz,
> córtanle el pie del estribo,   la mano del gavilán.[7]

Separation from hawks and hounds is symbolic of duress. The imprisoned Young Beichan (Child 53 H) sings about his great privations:

> "My hounds they all go masterless,
>   My hawks they flee frae tree to tree,
> My youngest brother will heir my lands,
>   My native land I'll never see."

In some versions of this ballad, his captor's daughter, helping him escape, supplies him with the basic necessities, including "a leash o guid gray-hounds" (Child 53 C, D). The boasting of knights at a revel, *Redesdale and Wise William* (Child 246 A), shows what is foremost in their minds:

> For some o them hae roosd their hawks,
>   And other some their hounds,
> And other some their ladies fair,
>   And their bowers whare they walkd in.

When Thomas Rhymer (Child 37) meets the Queen of Elfland, hawk and hounds are a part of her splendor:

> Her mantle was o velvet green,
>   And a' set round wi jewels fine;
> Her hawk and hounds were at her side,
>   And her bugle-horn in gowd did shine.

On the other hand, the Wild Huntsman's hawk and hound in a Danish ballad are appropriately black: "Suortte da ware hans høgge,/och suorte da varre hanns hund" (DgF 92).

It is not unusual for the hound and the hawk to display great virtue or for the latter to possess a moral stature superior to that of a human. In *The Three Ravens* (Child 26), the hawks and hounds are loyal to their master even after his death:

> "Downe in yonder greene field,
> There lies a knight slain under his shield.

> "His hounds they lie down at his feete,
> so well they can their master keepe.

> "His haukes they flie so eagerly,
> There's no fowle dare come him nie."

For the Serbians, a man's falcon is his protector and mentor. The falcon whose life Marko saved at Kossovo returns the kindness by bringing him water in his beak and shading him from the sun when he falls ill by the roadside.[8] Dmitar plans to poison his brother Bogdan during a feud over a horse and a falcon, but his falcon teaches him a lesson about the unity of brothers.[9] Lithuanians believed that killing a falcon brought disaster, since he was a friend and messenger of man; a ballad tells of a king who shoots a falcon and is mortally hit by the falling bird.[10] The greater elaboration of these details found in ballads of other countries contributes essentially to the understanding of brief, virtually lyric passages in the Spanish *Romancero,* such as that of the ominous hunt.

Even though hunting as a pastime can be found often enough in *romances* of the modern tradition, there is a certain tendency to omit this knightly occupation or to replace it with something closer to the modern singer's interests. Menéndez Pidal points out a change suffered by *Conde Dirlos.*[11] In the old minstrel ballad (*Prim.* 164), the count was an avid hunter:

> Estábase el conde Dirlos,   sobrino de don Beltrán,
> asentado en sus tierras,   deleitándose en cazar,
> cuando le vinieron cartas   de Carlos el emperante.

The letter contains the emperor's orders to go to war against the Moor Aliarde. Dirlos is especially loath to leave since he has been married less than a year, but the motif chosen to represent the end of the happy life is not the parting from his wife but the dismissal of his hunting companions:

> Triste estaba y pensativo,   no cesa de sospirar:
> despide los falconeros,   los monteros manda pagar,
> despide todos aquellos   con quien solía deleitarse.

In the modern version, the insertion of one letter switches the count's addiction from hunting to footwear, which, in turn, expands into a preceding verse about clothing and makes him into something of a fop:

> Estaba el conde Niño,   en su palacio real,
> deleitándose en vestir,   deleitándose en calzar,
> cuando le vinieron cartas   que tenía que marchar.[12]

Similar atrophy of the hunt motif can be observed in *La esposa infiel,* where the husband's hunting creates at home an occasion for adultery. In the versions collected in the sixteenth century, the lady tells the visiting knight that her husband is away hunting, whereupon the lover wishes destruction upon the husband, his hawk, and his hounds:

> —A caza es ido, a caza   a los montes de León.
> —Si a caza es ido, señora,   cáigale mi maldición,
> rabia le mate los perros,   aguilillas el falcón,
> lanzada de moro izquierdo   le traspase el corazón.
> (Prim. 136a)

A modern version from Asturias does retain hunting as the reason for the husband's absence, together with the curse, and even adds a third reference to the hunt by letting the husband arrive with game for the wife:

> —Mi marido es ido a caza   a los montes de León:
> para que no vuelva nunca,   le echaré una maldición:
> "Cuervos le saquen los ojos   águilas el corazón,
> los perros de mis rebaños   le arrastren en procesión."—
> Estando en estas palabras   el marido que llegó.
> —Ábreme la puerta, luna,   ábreme la puerta, sol,
> que te traigo un cervatillo   de los montes de León.—
> (Menéndez y Pelayo, 10:87)

However, the curse has undergone a typical change: gone are the inseparable companions of the medieval hunter—hawk and hounds—who in the old versions were to share the husband's misfortune. Pérez Vidal assumes that, with the coming of firearms, the original curse lost its gravity; in one of his examples from the Canary Islands, the hawk has been replaced by a ferret: "Cuervos le quiten los ojos,/aguelillas y hurón."[13] Nine of the ten variants from Santander published by Cossío and Maza coincide in the three references to hunting with the version from Asturias, above. The catch can be a rabbit, a bird, or three doves (1:215 ff.). Of the three Andalusian variants published by Menéndez y Pelayo, only in one is the husband said to be hunting and does he become the object of a curse by the wife, as is usual in the modern versions (in the early *romance*, the curse was pronounced by the lover). In one variant, "es ido a caza" has become "no 'stá en casa" (as also in a variant from the Canary Islands). The third Andalusian variant states only that the husband is out: "Que mi marido está fuera por esos montes de Dios'' (Menéndez y Pelayo, 10:179 ff.). This wording resembles that of the six Chilean variants published by Vicuña Cifuentes, in none of which does the wife say her husband is hunting.[14]

While the mention of hunting as an explanation of the husband's absence has become sporadic, the ballad singers have been reluctant to drop the curse, with its strong emotional effect, and they continue to use it in a modernized form to show the wife's depravity. As a contrast to her contemptible attitude, the husband's affection is expressed by the game he brings home—not just as a supplement to the diet, but as a personal favor to the wife (''que te traigo un conejito,'' ''que te traigo un pajarito''). That the latter two parts of the hunt motif—curse and gift—with their function of characterization are nowadays more important than the first reference to hunting is indicated by the variants that omit the business that has taken the husband away from home, but contain either the curse or the gift, or both.[15] The omission of the first mention of hunting must be due to changes both in actual custom and in the class that cultivates the *Romancero*. A knight most likely was either at war or on a pilgrimage, which could account for an absence of many years, or out hunting, which took him away for a short time.[16] A peasant—even a medieval and certainly a modern peasant—can have many chores away from home. Thus the ready association between ''out'' and ''hunting'' has faded, altering nothing in the plot of the *romance,* but depriving its style of some of its vigor. Adherence to the traditional preference for concrete images and action, together with the fact that hunting, though less prominently, is still within the scope of the experience of the ballad audience, may account for the retention of the pertinent lines in many texts of this *romance*, including some modern Portuguese and several Catalan variants of Castilian origin.[17]

Ballads of infidelity and treachery in several other countries specify the hunt as the reason for the husband's absence, as, for example, the Piedmontese *Donna Lombarda* and *Lucrezia.*[18] In the Scottish *Little Musgrave and Lady Barnard* (Child 81 G), the commonplace of hunting the fallow deer accounts for Lord Barnard's absence, which facilitates the meeting of his wife and Wee Messgrove:

> Lord Barnard's awa to the green wood,
> To hunt the fallow deer;
> His vassals a' are gane wi him,
> His companie to bear.

In the Portuguese *Morena,* the wife, impatient to visit her lover, the friar, urges the husband to go hunting:

> "Erguei-vos d'aí, homem meu   chamae os cães, ide a caça,
> que o mais certo coelho   é esse da madrugada,
> quo não ha caça mais certa   do que a da madrugada."[19]

Other mishaps besides adultery can occur at home while a man is out hunting. In several versions of *El cautivo,* the Moorish lady of the house (in Portuguese texts identified as the Moor's daughter) not only comforts the captive in the master's absence but also provides him with the means of escape.[20] In the Catalan *Nodriza,* the nurse falls asleep and lets the infant prince burn to a cinder while the king and the queen are hunting:

> Lo bon rey s' en va á cassá,   lo bon rey y la regina;
> no quede ningú al palau   sino l' infant y la dida.
>
> (Milá, p. 39)

Most often, however, the center of the trouble is the wife left at home by the hunter. Although most texts of the *romance* of the wicked mother-in-law fail to explain the man's absence at the outset, circumstantial evidence later indicates the hunt. As the mother-in-law sends the wife to her parents' home to have her first child, she promises to attend, upon the husband's return, to the hawk's needs:

> —Yo le daré de mi vino,   yo le daré de mi pan,
> cebada para el caballo,   carne para el gavilán.[21]

In some variants the mother-in-law promises to give either to her son or to his wife one-half of the bag:

> De la caza que él trujese   mandaréte la mitad;
> de la perdiz algo menos,   de la palomba algo más.[22]

Among other calamities a husband may find that his wife has been abducted during his hunt. Thus, *La esposa de don García*:

> Fuera a caza, fuera a caza   el infante don García,
> fuera a caza, fuera a caza,   no cazó como solía.
> Mientras tanto le llevaron   la su esposa doña Elvira.[23]

Abduction during the hunter's absence from home is particularly frequent in Russian *byliny* (epic ballads). Czar Koscheï, an unbeliever, seizes Mikhaïlo Potyk's wife; two nephews of the Lithuanian king take Prince Roman's sister.[24] The act can be reciprocal, as in the case of Prince Roman and Marya Yuryevna: while Roman is hunting, his wife is taken across the sea to Manuil; when Manuil rides out to hunt, Marya escapes and returns to her husband (Trautmann, pp. 369-71). Likewise, Czar Salomo is hunting when Torokashko arrives with his fabulous ships to abduct the czarina for Prince Vasily; Salomo, in pursuit of his wife, arrives, in turn, at Vasily's palace when the latter is out hunting (Trautmann, pp. 246, 248). In the Portuguese *Melisendra,* Gayfeiros rescues his wife while her captor is at a hunt:

> O rei que vinha da caça   la deitou a desfilar.
> Sentiu logo Dom Gayfeiros   como o iam alcançar.
> (Braga, *Romanceiro geral,* p. 101)

In a Sicilian ballad, the hunting trip of Scibilia's husband gives the Moors an opportunity to break down the door and take her away.[25] (Parallel to that, the husband has gone to war in a large group of European abduction ballads related to the Piedmontese *Moro Saracino* and the French *L'Escrivette.*)[26] A different combination of hunting and kidnapping occurs in *Las hijas del Conde Flores.* The Moorish queen asks her husband to go hunting and to bring her a Christian slave:

> —Sal a cazar, el rey moro,   a cazar como solías
> y traerásme una cristiana   de gran belleza y valía.
> Ya se saliera el rey moro   a las carreras salía
> y a la hija del buen conde   allí ficiera cautiva.[27]

The word *cazar* in this *romance* is interpreted by Daniel Devoto as *cautivar, capturar.*[28] On the other hand, "hunting" may have had a broad meaning of going out to take whatever was worth taking: the "hunt" could include a local raid, a skirmish, or an attack on wayfarers, as in this case.[29] Thus, in a Portuguese version, the Moors are sent to war for the same purpose:

> —A guerra, á guerra, mourinhos,   quero uma christã cativa.
> Uns vão pelo mar abaixo,   outros pela terra acima:

Tragam-me a christã cativa,   que é para a nossa rainha.
(Braga, *Romanceiro geral,* p. 103)

The two forms—*a cazar* and *a guerra*—lead in this *romance* to the same kind of action.

Since hunting is readily accepted as an explanation of a man's absence—as, for example, in the Portuguese *Promessa de noivado*[30]—it is natural to give it also as a false excuse. The king in the Portuguese *Condessa,* trying to conceal the execution of the boy from his mother, says his page has gone hunting:

> "Senhor rei que é do meu filho;   que eu o venho visitar?"
> "O seu filho é na caça,   é na caça, foi caçar."
> (Braga, *Açoriano,* p. 252)

In the Piedmontese *Parricida,* after Angelina has killed her father, the king, so that she could marry her lover, she tells her brother the father has gone hunting: " 'L papà l'è andáit a cassa, a cassa 'n sül Munfrá." The brother, more familiar with the details of hunting, begins to suspect foul play when he sees that the dogs are at home (Nigra, p. 88). The mother of the Danish Sir Oluf delays the disclosure of the news of his death to his bride in the same manner (DgF 47). In the corresponding Breton ballad, however, Count Nann's mother says he has gone to town.[31]

Similarly sporadic is the identification of a secondary figure as a hunter. In some versions of the German *Ulinger* and in *Die verkaufte Müllerin,* the brother, a hunter, either saves his sister or avenges her violent death.[32] The mother of Dom Pedro Pequenino receives the news of her son's imprisonment from a hunter (Braga, *Açoriano,* p. 257). A hunter tells the king that he saw the princess with Count Claros (*Prim.* 190), but a Portuguese version of the same *romance* gives the role of the tattler to a page (Braga, *Romanceiro geral,* p. 80), and, in the Scottish *Johnie Cock* (Child 114 A, D), the protagonist is betrayed to the foresters by an old palmer or a "silly auld man."

While hunt and hunter are, in their concreteness, more in keeping with best ballad style than would be an absence for undetermined reasons or the intervention of an unclassified agent, the fluctuations show that in the foregoing types of ballads they cannot be considered indispensable. We shall now come, however, to some special groups of ballads that derive from the hunt their distinguishing character.

One of the peculiar applications of the hunt is that of an allegory of love. The pursuit of a girl is described in the terminology of hunting—originally a learned conceit, but assimilated by the traditional poetry of many European countries and particularly frequent in France and Germany. In these songs the lyric element often predominates, and their rudimentary plot only conditionally warrants their inclusion in collections of narrative poems. The following song from the French Alps exemplifies the type:

> De (bon) matin je me prends, je me lève,
> A la chasse je suis allé;
> A la chasse des bécasses,
>   Dedans ce bois;
> J'ai rencontré une bergère
> Qui dormait.[33]

A Catalan song shows kinship to the French:

> Matinadas son fresquetas,   yo m' en vaig aná á cassá.
> . . . .
> No 'n trovo cassa ninguna   pera poderli atiná;
> hi ha sino una pastoreta   qu' en guardava bestiá.
> Ya l' en trovo adormideta   á la vora d' un canyá,
> yo 'n cullo un pom de violas   y al pit las hi vaig tirá.
>   (Milá, pp. 299-300)

The German versions often retain the time of early morning, but the girl is not identified as a shepherdess, and the song is not in the first but the third person:

> Es wollt' ein Jäger jagen
> Ein Hirschlein oder ein Reh,
> Drei Stündlein vor dem Tagen,
> Ein Hirschlein oder ein Reh.[34]

One of the rare Spanish examples of the love-hunt allegory calls the girl a white dove—a traditional metaphor in Spanish poetry:

> Me cogí la carabina   y al monte me fui a cazar,
> en el monte no cacé   porque nada pude hallar;
> sólo una blanca paloma,   en un rico palomar.
> La seguí hasta su casa,   por saber su voluntad,
> los padres que lo supieron,   la mandaron ocultar;

. . . .

> —No llores, blanca paloma,   no tienes por qué llorar,
> que en volviendo de soldado   contigo me he de casar.
>
> (Cossío and Maza, 2:84)

A variant of *La romera*—a *romance* about the Virgin Mary that makes use also of other mundane motifs involving combing and clothing—begins with the love-hunt:

> Iba el rey a cazar,   a cazar por alta sierra,
> en vez de encontrar caza   encontró una linda romera.
> Atrevido preguntóla,   si era casada o soltera.
> —Casadita soy, señor,   pero mi amor atrás queda.
>
> (Cossío and Maza, 2:148)

The love allegory lends itself to several local forms. In a Russian *bylina*, Mikhaïlo Potyk aims his arrow at a white swan that is swimming on the sea, but the bird asks him not to shoot since she is really a beautiful maiden; he takes her along on his horse and marries her (Trautmann, p. 314). Here the allegory is closely related to the type of *bylina* where a bird gives useful advice to a hunter after asking him to spare its life.[35] In a Polish song, the girl is a part of the catch that two hunters divide: "Rabbit and deer for you; sable and girl for me."[36] A Lithuanian song, presumably also of Polish origin, deals with a hunter who finds no game but discovers a girl asleep in the meadow and tells her it is a hunter's custom to kiss a girl found in the woods (Balys, p. 137).

In Denmark, where metaphoric dialogue is not alien to traditional ballads, it is hardly surprising that in a conversation between the king and Terkel Trundesøn the hunt stands for courtship:

> "I rode to the wood with hawk and hound,
>   The game for a while I chased,
> And every sportsman, who hunts the deer,
>   Is tempted the time to waste."

The king, who does not approve of the match between Terkel and Adelus, Sir Lave's daughter, replies:

> "Thou ridest so long in greenwood shaw
>   A chasing Sir Lave's game,
> The deer, thou lovest so well to chase,

The hunter himself will maim.''
(DgF 480, trans. Prior, 2:450)

The substitution of hunting for wooing was apparently common usage, assimilated by conversational language, from where it passed into ballads.[37] It can be found even in Spanish and Portuguese *romances,* where literary metaphors are scarce. Thus, Gerenaldo, after trysting with the princess, tells the king:

"Venho de caçar a rôla   da outra banda do rio.''
"A rôla que tu caçaste   já t'a tinha promettido.''
(Braga, *Açoriano,* p. 267)

Count Claros overrules in like language the lady's attempt to postpone a tryst:

—Bien sabedes vos, señora,   que soy cazador real;
caza que tengo en la mano   nunca la puedo dejar.—
Tomárala por la mano,   para un vergel se van.
(*Prim.* 190)

The evolution—or perhaps degeneration—of the love-hunt, as it was absorbed by folk song and transformed in the process, exemplifies strikingly the difference between learned and popular poetry. John Meier points out that in medieval artistic poems, where it originated, the allegory was carried out consistently until the end. But when the motif was adopted (fourteenth to sixteenth century) and transmitted by popular songs, successive changes led to a precipitate identification of the game—usually a hind—as a girl, which rendered the subsequent description of high leaps, and so on, absurd:

Er jagt wohl durch ein grünes Gestrauch,
Er jagt ein schwarzbraunes Mädel heraus,

"Du bist ein Jäger und fangst mich nicht,
Weißt du meine krumme Sprünge noch nicht.''
(Meier, *Balladen,* 2:238)

Meier observes further that the symbolic terminology of the hunt ("shooting" and "bringing down") came to be taken literally, and, as a result, the original ending—acceptance or rejection of the suitor—was changed into the death of the girl.[38] This change in the interpretation is quite in keeping with the conventions of popular ballad language, where an object or action, while it may signify a broader concept, usually retains also its literal meaning. There is no doubt that the folk songs in question were understood to deal with an amorous pursuit; but also the hunt itself became a reality, and the conquest of the girl by the hunter, formerly symbolized by his bagging the game, turned into a killing of the girl.

In many ballads, the change from deer into girl is altogether omitted. The hunter goes into the forest and finds a girl, as in some of the songs quoted at the beginning of this section or in DgF 230 C, where a knight finds a maid in the forest, has to walk while she rides his horse, and, upon arrival at her home, is left behind the door. The outcome is the same in the Piedmontese *Monacella salvata,* where a hunter is left waiting under an olive tree by a nun who flees into the convent under the pretext of discarding her habit (Nigra, p. 444). In the same category is the version of the Spanish *Caballero burlado* that begins with a hunting scene borrowed from *La infantina encantada* (Cossío and Maza, 1:119). But the introductory hunt is not an integral part of these pastourelles. The story of *El caballero burlado*—a girl gets a free ride on the croup and keeps the knight at arm's length by pretending to be a child of lepers—does not mention a hunter in the version known as *La hija del rey de Francia* ("De Francia partió la niña," *Prim.* 154, 154a). The theme occurs without the hunt motif also in the Piedmontese *Occasione mancata* (Nigra, p. 438) and in the British *Baffled Knight* (Child 112). Evidently the sportive story—a complete ballad in its own right—attracted in many countries the similarly playful motif of the love-hunt.[39]

However, the countries that produced the combinations of the love-hunt and humorous ballads, use some form of the hunt motif also to preface tragic themes. A Danish song (DgF 416) at first coincides with that of the baffled suitor (DgF 230 C, above), but then develops into a fight between the knight and the girl's seven brothers, in which all of the men die. The Piedmontese *Fuga* (Nigra, p. 125) begins with a repartee between a lion-hunting prince and a coquettish shepherdess, but ends in her suicide with his sword—a commonplace in abduction ballads, as *Il Corsaro* (Nigra, p. 119).

A further example of the great popularity of the love-hunt is found by Erich Seemann in a Dutch version of *Der Spielmannssohn*—originally the story of a fiddler who escapes the gallows and marries a princess—where the lover of the princess is now called a hunter (*Deutsche Volkslieder*, 3:176). Even the unrelated motif of a baby being found by hunters (cf. DgF 293, 294) is combined in a Lithuanian ballad with the love-hunt: a hunter finds a baby girl in a brazen cradle, swings the cradle, and kisses the girl; when she grows up, she is not willing to marry anyone but him (Balys, p. 71).

The numerous—and sometimes incongruous—graftings of the love-hunt motif to various stories show some common traits: (1) The plot of the ballad can be any kind of love story, from flirtation to high tragedy; (2) in most cases, the love-hunt has lost the characteristics of an allegory; a hunter simply finds a girl; (3) a remnant of the degenerated love-hunt allegory is the occasional implicit or explicit statement that the hunter has found no game ("en vez de encontrar caza   encontró una linda romera"). The reason is given plainly in a French song:

> Quand je vais à la chasse,
> Ce n'est pas pour chasser,
> C'est pour aller voir ma tant joli' bergère
> Qui est la bas
> Couché, sur la fougère.
>
> (Tiersot, p. 381)

The girl is the game that the hunter sets out to catch in the first place.

The suppression of the overt elements of the allegory brings the love-hunt deceptively close to a realistic image, but—although the possibility of meeting a girl during a hunt cannot be ruled out completely—the motif, even in its briefest form, must be considered an outgrowth of a literary invention. In comparison with other motifs, such as the hunt as a reason for absence from home, the amount of corroboration from real-life experience would be slight. The strength of the motif lies in its lyric aspect, which accounts for its widespread use and long survival.

The contracted form of the love-hunt does not achieve its effect through the intellectual exercise that was the basis of the original allegory, but through a subconscious transfer of the characteristics of the hunt to the courtship. The dynamic quality of the chase reverberates in the hunter's wooing; the flight of the game, in the girl's evasiveness. The brevity of the motif leaves no time to solve the mathematical equation; the two images are superimposed, and, thus, often confused.

Through a different process, the hunt motif has become also an introduction to death. This form is highly typical of the Hispanic *Romancero,*
yet can best be understood with the help of the more detailed and coherent
narrative found in ballads of other countries. While the lyric association
of hunting and courtship was originally an intellectually conceived allegory, the association of hunting and death—equally lyric in its final stage
of evolution—has some of its roots in reality, since the hunt used to be a
likely occasion for a man to be killed by his enemies. Well-known in epic
songs, such as the *Nibelungenlied,* the motif of violent death during a hunt
occurs also in ballads.

In *Landarico,* the king surprises the queen in her room before he goes
hunting:

> Para ir el rey a caza   de mañana ha madrugado,
> entró donde está la reina   sin la haber avisado.

The queen, assuming the visitor is her lover Landarico, inadvertently gives
away the secret; to protect herself and Landarico, she has the king assassi-
nated at his return from the hunt in the dark:

> Llama a un criado suyo   hombre de muy bajo estado,
> que mate al rey, le dice   en habiéndose apeado,
> que sería a boca de noche   cuando oviese tornado.
> (Menéndez y Pelayo, 9:219)

Menéndez y Pelayo (12:488-92) finds in the *Historia Francorum* that King
Chilpericus was murdered in the year 584, at his return from a hunt at
nightfall. Popular opinion attributed the crime to his wife and her lover
Landericus. An analogous case is the German *Frau von Weißenburg,* presumably based on the murder of the Palatine Friedrich von Goseck in 1085
during a hunt. His death likewise was instigated by his wife and her lover,
whom she married after the obligatory period of mourning. Several variants of the ballad deviate from the chronicle: the lover has to commit the
murder with his own hands, since his squire refuses to do it; then, after
showing the bloody dagger to the lady, he forsakes her (*Deutsche
Volkslieder,* 1:301 ff.). Whether or not these and similar ballads reflect
historical events, a hunt would be a convenient setting for a murder. Child
finds no record of the specific incident of *The Death of Parcy Reed* (Child
193), but points out that "almost every circumstance in the narrative exists
in tradition" (4:24). Moreover, the practical details of the preparation for

the slaying give the ballad the appearance of a real event: Parcy's enemies invite him to go hunting; when he falls asleep after a tiring day, they put water in his gun, steal his powder horn, jam his sword into the sheath—making it easy for a band of mosstroopers to kill him. No details of the apprehension of the king are given in the Piedmontese *Re prigionero*; evidently the vulnerability of a hunter is taken for granted: "Lo re Luis no va a la cassa, no va a la cassa anturn d'Paris. / S'a l'àn pià-ro, l'àn lià-ro, l'àn mnà'lo 'nt la tur d' Paris" (Nigra, p. 64).

In Danish ballads family feuds reach a bloody settlement when the hostile parties meet in the woods. Three ballads end with a fatal clash between the hero and the lady's brothers, whose permission to court their sister he has failed to ask (DgF 303, 415, 416). In the first two, Hjelmer and Oluf are further guilty of having slain either the father or an uncle of the youths and not paid the prescribed fine.

In all the foregoing ballads, the hunt is a circumstance that allows the catastrophe to occur, but without an accumulation of omens that would presage a disaster. On the other hand, the Spanish *romances*, often dealing with very similar subjects, use the hunt to build up dramatic tension and to create by means of a few details an atmosphere that foreshadows the main event. Such is the hunt of don Rodrigo de Lara, who is involved in a blood feud, similar to that of the Danish ballads, for having caused the death of his seven nephews:

> A caça va don Rodrigo,   esse que dizen de Lara;
> perdido avía los açores,   no halla ninguna caça;
> con la gran siesta que hace   arrimóse a una haya.[40]

These verses express in a capsule the doom of the hunter. He has lost his falcons—not only invaluable aids in hunting, but, as shown previously, the emblems of a knight, participants in his character and fate, sometimes endowed with supernatural powers of protecting their master. He has found no game; he has been marked as a loser. He leans against a beech tree; evidently he is alone and weary, but his withdrawal from the active chase means also that he is giving up the control of events; he turns himself over to fate. Under these circumstances, his vow to kill Mudarra is not a promise but a last, futile protest. When Mudarra arrives, with a courteous greeting and a formal introduction, he has the role of an executor of a death sentence, already pronounced.[41] In the more concise variants, the *romance* ends with the imminent, not the accomplished, fact: "Aquí morirás, traidor,   enemigo de doña Sancha.''[42] Since the introductory verses have determined don Rodrigo's fate, there is no doubt as to the outcome.

Menéndez Pidal, reconstructing the epic of the *Infantes de Salas* from chronicles, points out the process of poetic selection. The unfortunate hunt was a detailed incident in the epic: don Rodrigo sent his falcon after a heron, but both birds disappeared in the clouds; while he and his men searched for the falcon, the troops of his pursuer arrived and engaged in a fight with those of don Rodrigo.[43] The *romance* makes of the mass scene an intimate encounter between two enemies; the ominous hunt and the loneliness of the hunter reinforce each other in the creating of an atmosphere of inevitable fate.

Very similar is the beginning of a *romance* from a different cycle, *La penitencia de don Rodrigo,* in a modern version from Asturias:

> Don Rodrigo fue a caza,   a caza como solía.
> Non encontró cosa muerta   nin tampoco cosa viva.
> La traidora de la muerte   n'el camino le salía.
> ¡Ay de mí, triste isgraciadol   yo confesarme quería.
> *(Romancero tradicional,* 1:72)

The sixteenth-century text (*Prim.* 7) says nothing about a hunt; the king, through whose fault the realm has fallen into Moorish hands, is shown as a fugitive:

> Después que el rey don Rodrigo   a España perdido había,
> íbase desesperado   por donde más le placía.
> Métese por las montañas   las más espesas que había,
> porque no le hallen los moros   que en su seguimiento iban.

Like the final episode of the cycle of the *Infantes de Salas,* this is a story of a guilty man, about to meet his just punishment. *La penitencia de don Rodrigo,* in the late version, has lost most of the rambling narrative of the minstrel ballad; it highlights the king's penance—being buried alive with a snake. The initial verses have developed into a variant of the dismal hunt, which retains the mood of loneliness and despair, but, at the same time, signals the point of no return: King Rodrigo fails to see anything, dead or alive, on his path; he has been expelled from the world.

The addition of the hunt motif cannot be dismissed as a simple case of mobility of a commonplace, attracted—one might say—by the name

Rodrigo. Not only does the dismal hunt express more forcefully the mood discernible in the earlier introduction, but the elements that are condensed into the poetic motif in the previous two ballads can be found in other, similar situations in a low-keyed form. Thus, another guilty king, Pedro el Cruel, receives during a hunt the message of doom:

> Por los campos de Jerez   a caza va el rey don Pedro;
> en llegando a una laguna,   allí quiso ver un vuelo.
> Vido volar una garza,   desparóle un sacre nuevo,
> remontárale un neblí,   a sus pies cayera muerto.
> A sus pies cayó el neblí,   túvolo por mal agüero.
> Tanto volaba la garza,   parece llegar al cielo.
>
> *(Prim.* 66a)

From the point where the heron rises, descends a shepherd, weeping and sighing. He is hairy all over, unkempt, his feet full of thorns; he carries a snake, a bloody dagger, a shroud, a skull, and has a black dog on a leash. After enumerating don Pedro's crimes, he prophesies a violent death and then disappears. This systematic list of omens, accompanied by an explanation, is, in essence, a counterpart of the dismal hunt.

Somewhat similar is the Danish "long ballad" of *Marsk Stig,* about King Erik, who has abducted Lady Ingeborg, the wife of the marshal. Ingeborg's nephew, Ranild, entices the king to go hunting and leads him along a lonely road:

> They hunted stag, they hunted hind,
>   They chased the fleeting roe,
> They stay'd so long, that at the last
>   They saw the daylight go.
>   (DgF 145, trans. Prior, 2:205)

They find a hut, with a cheerful fire and a lovely maid inside. The maid laughs off the king's amorous overture, makes an enigmatic prophecy about the length of his life, and vanishes together with her cozy abode. The king is then led by Ranild to a barn and slain by Lady Ingeborg's men. Prior observes that "the phantasm in the wood . . . is certainly one of the finest impersonations of a guilty conscience to be found in the whole range of ballad poetry" (2:195-96). Considering the clerical origins of many ballads, such an interpretation is not baseless. At the same time, the uncanny maid blends easily into the host of fairy creatures that inhabit the woods and are wont to step into a hunter's path. This happens, for example, to Tam Lin (Child 39 A):

> "And ance it fell upon a day.
>   A cauld day and a snell,
> When we were frae the hunting come,
>   That frae my horse I fell;
> The Queen o Fairies she caught me,
>   In yon green hill to dwell."

Also the Danish Dwarf-King's daughter, who binds Sir Tønne with the music of her golden harp, appears to him during a hunt (DgF 34).

Surprisingly the hunt motif, though very frequent in Denmark, crops up only sporadically, and in a very brief form, in variants of *Elveskud* (DgF 47)—a ballad that has Breton and Spanish counterparts in which the hero's hunt plays an important role.[44] The Breton Count Nann sets out to get venison for his wife, who has given birth to twins; he follows a white hind until nightfall and dismounts to drink from a spring, where he finds a *korrigan* (forest fairy) combing her hair with a golden comb; since he refuses to marry her, he must die, but his death is kept secret from his wife until she discovers it on the day of her churching (La Villemarqué, p. 25). While the second part—the delay of the news of the death—contains the same elements in most European versions, the hero's death is given different causes. In France, he usually comes home from war mortally wounded (*Le roi Renaud,* Doncieux, p. 87). As Doncieux points out, the French singers have stripped the Breton *gwerz* of all the marvelous elements.[45] Even where the hero returns from a hunt with a fatal injury, as in the Piedmontese *Morte occulta* (E), the event does not pass the limits of reality: "Ven da la cassa lo re Rinald, ven da la cassa, l'è tüt ferì."[46] A Sephardic version of the corresponding Spanish *romance, La muerte ocultada,* does contain a supernatural occurrence, but quite different from the one in the Breton ballad:

> Levantóse Uezo   lunes de mañana,
> tomara sus armas,   fuérase a la caza.
> En un prado verde   sentóse a almorzare;
> allí viera Uezo   muy negra señale . . .
> Firió Uezo al Huerco   en el calcañale,
> firió el Huerco a Uezo   en su voluntade;
> firió Uezo al Huerco   con su rica espada,
> firió el Huerco a Uezo   en telas del alma.[47]

Menéndez Pidal believes that Huerco (the Latin Orcus, god of death and the underworld) belongs to the early peninsular versions of this *romance*. Derivatives of the word *huerco* used in Asturias and Galicia refer to a harbinger of death, which appears in various forms—white or black dog, specter, wraith.[48] The motif has undergone several mutations. In one variant, a process of rationalization has changed a letter in the word and made of the spirit a pig or boar (*puerco*):

> Estando don Hueso   un día a cazar,
> de que no vido a nadie   se puso a merendar.
> Y ya que vido un puerco   emporcando el río,
> se levantó don Hueso   y le ha tirado un tiro:
> al puerco le ha dado   en el corbejón,
> y a don Hueso le ha dado   en el corazón.
> (Menéndez Pidal, "Romancero
> judío-español," p. 166)

In modern versions from Asturias, don Pedro is stricken with fatal illness during his hunt:

> A cazar iba don Pedro,   a cazar como solía,
> los perros lleva cansados   y el halcón perdido había.
> Diérale el mal de la muerte;   para casa se volvía.
> (Menéndez y Pelayo, 10:111)

Or he meets Death personified:

> A cazar iba don Pedro   por esos montes arriba;
> caminara siete leguas   sin encontrar cosa viva,
> si no fuera cuervos negros,   que los perros no querían.
> Apeóse a descansar   al pie de una seca encina;
> caía la nieve a copos   y el agua menuda y fría.
> Allegósele la Muerte   a tenerle compañía.[49]

The last two variants show a marked similarity to the *romances* of the death of don Rodrigo de Lara and the penitence of King Rodrigo, above. The original episode of action has been replaced by a lyric motif. Life quietly turns away from the hunter in the solitude of a mysterious forest. One by one the positive, vital elements of his existence desert him: no game in sight; dogs tired; falcon lost; his own strength ebbing; instead of sunlight, snow and freezing rain.[50] Compared with this dark, ominous silence, the fight with Huerco during the lunch hour seems much more matter-of-fact, almost rational; even though he ends up as the loser, the man has at least a chance to defend himself. In the later versions there is no fight, no action. Alone and weary at the foot of an oak—and even the oak is dry—man succumbs to an invisible enemy.

The poetic image of the approach of death evidently became preferable and, consequently, displaced the narrative in *La muerte ocultada* as it displaced the explanation of the aimless wandering of King Rodrigo. The dismal hunt, which only in *Don Rodrigo de Lara* seems to be a direct outgrowth of the facts in the original story, has become a suggestive introduction, deemed suitable for many *romances* that deal with death.

The connection between the hunting scene and the narrative seems at first glance very loose in *Rico Franco* (*Prim.* 119):

> A caza iban, a caza   los cazadores del rey,
> ni fallaban ellos caza,   ni fallaban qué traer.
> Perdido habían los halcones   ¡mal los amenaza el rey!
> Arrimáranse a un castillo   que se llamaba Maynés.
> Dentro estaba una doncella   muy fermosa y muy cortés;
> siete condes la demandan,   y así facían tres reyes.
> Robárala Rico Franco,   Rico Franco aragonés.

Bénichou (*Romancero,* p. 161) points out that, to tie the two parts together, one has to assume that the abductor Rico Franco was one of the hunters, even though this is neither stated nor implied in the *romance*; he further points out that the Sephardic version is even more incoherent, letting the father give his much-wooed daughter to a *rico fraile.* The lack of logical sequence appears to have caused an erroneous classification of this *romance.* It is customary to include *Rico Franco* in the long list of European ballads of the *Lady Isabel and the Elf-Knight* and the *Halewijn-Ulinger* group, since the abducted girl kills Rico Franco with his own knife—a denouement which coincides with a prominent version of the European group mentioned. One might assume that the European story attracted in Spain the hunting scene, the latter being a favorite introduction to *romances* that end in death.

At closer scrutiny, however, *Rico Franco* has more in common with the German *Bluthochzeit,* a ballad of considerable age, found in the Rhine area and among German settlers in Transylvania:

> Frühmorgens der Pfalzgraf zum Waidwerk reit',
> viel Diener und Knappen in seinem Geleit.

Or, another variant:

Es fuhr sich ein Pfalzgraf wohl über den Rhein
Viel Roß und Jäger wohl um ihn sein.
(*Deutsche Volkslieder,* 2:159)

In some versions the girl is a princess; in some newer ones, a miller's daughter. The Count Palatine kills her parents and three brothers, and takes her along against her will—two important details that appear in *Rico Franco,* but are not found in the *Halewijn* series. There is no indication that Rico Franco is more than an abductor by force; he is not shown to have any natural or supernatural appeal like that of the elf-knight, Halewijn, or their human successors in balladry, which would lure the girl into his power. In fact the killing of the abductor by the girl is the only major motif that sets *Rico Franco* apart from *Bluthochzeit,* where the girl becomes the abductor's wife.[51] Those German *Bluthochzeit* texts that begin with the Palatine's hunt show a resemblance to *Rico Franco* precisely in a detail that distinguishes the hunt motif from the usual form in each country: the hunters are many ("los cazadores del rey," "viel Diener und Knappen in seinem Geleit," "viel Roß und Jäger wohl um ihn sein"). In other Spanish *romances* where the hunt leads to death, the hunter is alone; likewise alone is the stereotyped German hunter who finds a girl in the forest. Thus the foreign ballad that inspired *Rico Franco* was not necessarily a member of the *Halewijn* group, but possibly a version of *Bluthochzeit,* on which the girl's revenge was grafted. A similar denouement is found also in other Spanish *romances,* such as *Venganza de honor* or *Hija de la viudina,* and is perhaps more in keeping with the poetic justice favored in the *Romancero.* The initial brief hunt motif may have assimilated the typically Spanish elaboration of the unlucky hunt—not finding any game, losing the falcons. Considering that the Spanish version concludes with the death of the abductor, the ominous hunt has to the main theme an undeniable, though irrational, affinity.

The introductory motif of the unlucky hunt would be comparable to a prologue in the theater or an emblematic song that creates the appropriate mood in the audience before the curtain rises. The purpose of the hunt motif is to suggest that the protagonist has entered the realm of an unknown fate against which he is powerless. This impression is achieved in two ways simultaneously: the failure in the hunt symbolizes the hunter's defeat in the subsequent action, and the association of the hunt and the dark forest with many kinds of supernatural beings (some of these have been and others will be discussed) evokes the presence of unfathomable

forces. In the light of the hunter's fight with Huerco = Orcus in the Sephardic *romance,* the forest may also represent a mythical underworld.

Outside Spain one can find some of the component parts of the ominous
hunt, as, for example, in the silver wood where Child Maurice (Child 83 A)
hunts and is later slain by his mother's husband:

> Childe Maurice hunted ithe siluer wood,
>   He hunted itt round about,
> And noebodye *that* he ffound therin,
>   Nor none there was with-out.

The foresters take Johnie Cock (Child 114) by surprise as he and his
hounds are in deep sleep after drinking the blood of a dun deer. The scene
somewhat resembles the rest in the woods and the vulnerability of some
Spanish protagonists, but Johnie's hunt was successful and there is no
clear hint of a participation by supernatural powers, even though the latter
could be easily attributed to the dun deer.

An animal, usually an elusive deer, is in many European ballads something more than it seems to the hunter who begins to chase it. The white
hind that lures Count Nann, in the Breton ballad, to the *korrigan*'s abode
is undoubtedly a messenger from fairyland.[52] The long *Marqués de
Mantua* is tantalizingly noncommittal as to the nature of the deer that appears to the hunters while they are resting in a grove. They release their
hounds and rush after the game; at nightfall, the marquis finds himself
alone in a dense forest, caught in a thunderstorm; he blows his horn, but
his companions are too far off to hear it; he gives his stumbling horse free
rein; a cry of pain rends the air; after cutting his way through the thicket,
the marquis finds his beloved nephew Valdovinos close to death. This
romance contains in dilated form several of the elements that make up the
familiar ominous hunt motif, with some meaningful complements. Even
before the lonely hunter is overtaken by night and ill weather, there are
some verses that according to the conventions of the *Romancero,* point
toward an extraordinary—possibly supernatural—event: they tell us that
the hunt takes place on the seashore on the Eve of Saint John:

> De Mantua salió el marqués   Danés Urgel el leal:
> allá va a buscar la caza   a las orillas del mar.
> . . . .

El tiempo era caluroso, víspera era de Sant Juan.
(Prim. 165)

Considering the context, the escaping deer also is in all likelihood meant to be of supernatural character, but the *Romancero* seldom identifies its pagan complements explicitly.

There is, on the other hand, no doubt that the hog that appears before Fernán Gonzàlez is a divine messenger:

> El conde Fernán González cabe la villa de Lara,
> mientra la gente se junta sálese a buscar la caza.
> Dentro en los robles del monte un puerco se levantara,
> tras él arremete el conde de los suyos se alejaba.
> (Menéndez y Pelayo, 9:180)

The hog takes refuge at the altar in a hermitage; Fernán González is met by a monk in white robes who foretells the victory over Almanzor; after the prophecy has come true, Fernán González gives his share of the booty to build the church of San Pedro de Arlanza. J. P. Keller relates this *romance* to legends of saints that tell of animals bearing a flaming cross on the forehead, as, for example, the deer that appeared to Saint Eustace.[53] Also in other ballads one can find animals with religious credentials. Digenis, the Greek hero, tells his friends he has to die because he killed a deer that had a cross on the antlers, a star on the head, and on the shoulder blade a likeness of the Holy Virgin.[54] A particular type of animal is the hare that Jenus and Nilus are chasing on Easter Sunday in the Danish *Helligbrøden* (DgF 112). The hare foretells Nilus's failure in the hunt and the death of his comrade; indeed, the friends kill each other in a quarrel, and even their hounds follow suit.[55] The subject matter of this ballad exists also in Basque folklore in Spain. *Eiztari-beltza* (the black hunter)—a species of the Wild Huntsman active on stormy nights—is a priest who has left his Mass unfinished to join his hounds in the chase of a hare and is condemned to run forever, without reaching the game. The hare is sometimes said to be the devil himself, at other times a witch.[56]

But the Christian reinterpretation, which made of the ancient Woden's chase an aid to sermons, has failed to reach many other kinds of marvelous hunts and animals. The deer in the Scandinavian *Harpens Kraft* (DgF 40), which lures all the members of the wedding procession away, letting the bride fall into the hands of a watersprite, is clearly in the service of the non-Christian world of nature spirits. In a Bulgarian ballad, also, a deer appears to a wedding party and ushers in the catastrophe: the bridegroom, left alone with the bride, tries to kiss her (in other variants, to free her veil from a branch or to cut an apple); his knife, or sword, disengages itself and wounds the bride fatally (*Deutsche Volkslieder,* 2:210). In a German epic the hero, Wolfdietrich, and his men set out to chase a deer whose antlers are wound with gold, sent to them by the knight Drasian, who uses the opportunity to abduct Wolfdietrich's wife Sigeminne (*Deutsche Volkslieder,* 5:41-42).

In the *Romancero* there is a certain ambivalence toward such prodigious deer. On the one hand the minstrels were obviously attracted to the motif, but at the same time they played down the pagan connections. In *Eneas y Dido* (*Prim.* 110)—doubtless the work of somebody familiar with the *Aeneid*—the hunters rush after a swift deer and leave the protagonists alone:

> Eneas que esto contaba,   un ciervo que parecía:
> echó mano a su aljaba,   una saeta le tira.
> El golpe le dio en vano,   el ciervo muy bien corría.
> Pártense los cazadores,   síguelo el que más podía;
> la reina Dido y Eneas   quedaron sin compañía.

In Vergil's poem, Juno's scheme for uniting Aeneas and Dido includes sending bountiful game that would keep the beaters occupied; an added feature in the Spanish ballad is the particular deer. Yet there is no indication that the animal was dispatched by the goddess. This deer and the one in the *Marqués de Mantua* are typical examples of the equivocal supernatural element in the *Romancero*—possibly an intermediate stage between the marvelous and the rational, as well as a compromise between classical scholarship and Christian doctrine.

As an exception, the *Romance de Lanzarote* has retained the magic character of its Breton heritage:

> Tres hijuelos había el rey,   tres hijuelos, que no más;
> por enojo que hubo de ellos   todos maldito los ha.
> El uno se tornó ciervo,   el otro se tornó can,
> el otro se tornó moro,   pasó las aguas del mar.

Also the dangers surrounding the white-footed deer are recorded in the same *romance*:

Por aquí pasó esta noche   dos horas antes del día,
siete leones con él   y una leona parida.
Siete condes deja muertos   y mucha caballería.[57]

Transformation into an animal, rare in the *Romancero*, is a common occurrence in European balladry. In *The Three Ravens* (Child 26), the fallow doe is identified as the slain knight's leman:

> Downe there comes a fallow doe,
> As great with yong as she might goe.
>
> She lift vp his bloudy hed,
> And kist his wounds that were so red.
>
> She got him vp vpon her backe,
> And carried him to earthen lake.
>
> She buried him before the prime,
> She was dead herselfe ere even-song time.
>
> God send euery gentleman,
> Such haukes, such hounds, and such a leman.

There is a hint of the same phenomenon in the request the lady makes of Leesome Brand (Child 15) to "hunt the deer and roe" while she gives birth to their child, but not to touch the white hind, "for she is o the woman kind." He hunts with such pleasure that he forgets the lady, until he sees the milk-white hind, turns back, and finds both mother and child dead.[58] The identity of the white hind is clearly stated in the French *Marguerite ou la blanche biche*:

> "J'ai bien grande ire en mois,   et n'ose vous le dire:
> Je sui fille sur jour   et la nuit blanche biche.
> La chasse est après moi,   les barons et les princes."
> (Doncieux, p. 235)

Renaud does not heed his mother's plea to refrain from chasing the white hind; the slain animal is found to have blond hair and the breast of a girl; when Renaud, back in the castle, asks for his sister, she speaks to him from a dish on the banquet table. Doncieux believes this poem is to be traced to a prototype from Scandinavia, where, indeed, such ballads abound. Besides *Jomfruen i Hindeham* (DgF 58), partly the same as the French story, there is one about a girl changed by her stepmother into a white hind, who, to escape the hounds of her fiancé, Sir Orm, turns into a hawk, recovering her human shape when Sir Orm offers her a slice of flesh from his own breast (DgF 56). In another ballad, the stepmother turns the brother into a wolf, the sister into a nightingale; the brother regains his human form by drinking the stepmother's blood; the sister, hers by a series of transformations similar to those of Tam Lin (Child 39), culminating in a cut by her brother's knife (DgF 57). Another maid is turned by her stepmother into scissors, a swordblade, and finally a werewolf, and casts off the spell by drinking her unborn stepbrother's blood (DgF 55). Besides such gory sacrifices, there is a different method of disenchantment: the youth kisses a linden tree and turns it back into a beautiful maiden, who has likewise been a victim of her stepmother (DgF 66). Most of the time, however, kissing is equal to a heroic act, since the temporary shape is anything but inviting. Signelill has to kiss a dragon (DgF 65), Jenus to embrace a snake, in order to unspell a prospective mate (DgF 59). Thus, disenchantment is accomplished by courage and by love, or perhaps more precisely, by the courage to love.

The large group of ballads about disenchantment has a somewhat anomalous representative in Spain: *La infantina encantada.* In most texts, the girl has not been changed into an animal. Only the Catalan version tells of a deer who—drinking from a spring on the night of Saint John—asks the hunter not to shoot but to marry her, since she is a girl enchanted by her father for a year and a day:

> Al passant d' un' arboleda   qu' es [arboleda] molt linda;
> que las truncas son de *oro,*   las ramas de plata fina;
> al mitx d' aquell' arboleda   n' hi ha una font tan linda,
> a n'el mitx d' aquella font   [n' hi ha] un cérvol que hi bevía:
> "Cassadó, 'l bon cassadó,   *mírame* y no me tiris,
> no som cérvol, cassadó,   no som cérvol que som nina,
> qu' el meu *padre* m' ha encantada   sols per un any y un dia."
>
> (Milá, p. 174)

The hunter wants to ask his mother for advice, and the deer-girl utters the imprecation usual in this *romance.* In a short version, the girl is a snake drinking from a fountain:

> No so serp que so una *niña,*
> yo seré la tev' aymía   de la nit fins en el dia.

Mes a-luego no podría,   el meu pare ho sabría.
(Milá, p. 174)

There is no speaking animal in the Spanish and Portuguese versions. The *romance* begins with a shorter or longer form of the dismal hunt motif— hounds tired, falcon lost, nightfall, sometimes also snow and freezing rain, a weary hunter resting against a tree. The tree is of gold and silver; as the hunter lifts his eyes, he sees on the highest bough a beautiful girl combing her long hair with a golden comb. A Sephardic version unites most of the significant features:

A cazar iba el caballero,   a cazar como solía,
los perros iban cansados   y el halcón perdido había.
¿Ánde le cogió la noche?   En una oscura *montina*
ande canta la leona   y el león le respondía,
ande cae la nieve a copos   y corría el agua fría.
En el asomàrase a un pino,   alto es a maravilla,
la raíz es de oro   y las hojas de plata fina:
en el pimpollo más alto   vido estar a una infantita:
cabello de su cabeza   todo aquel roble cubría,
los ojos de la su cara   la montaña esclarecían,
los dientes de la su boca   aljófares parecían.[59]

The girl tells the knight she has been enchanted by seven fairies, but now her seven years are up and she is ready to go with him as wife, mistress, or slave. The faint-hearted knight hurries home to ask his mother for advice, and finds on his return that the infanta has been carried off by somebody else. For his failure, he decrees his own punishment, usually tantamount to death.

The *Infantina encantada* is a fusion of several ballad themes and motifs: (1) A hunter fails in his hunt—the typically Spanish dismal hunt motif; (2) a hunter finds a girl—a contraction of the love-hunt allegory; (3) a girl, combing her hair, is waiting for a man; (4) an enchanted girl expects to be saved through love; (5) a man fails because of indecision. Despite the conventionality of the separate parts, there is an unresolved discord in the combination. The unlucky hunt, which usually heralds death, may seem at first glance misplaced, since the knight's tragedy is his failure to find the infanta, not his rhetorical exclamation about the death that he feels he deserves. In fact the latter is missing in some shorter versions. In any case this slight—and only seeming—inconsistency will be explained shortly. The most stymieing question is: Why does the hunter hesitate?[60]

One might say that he knew the infanta to be a fairy, sitting in the middle of a lonely forest as she was, combing her long hair with a golden comb and offering herself with the sole condition of being taken along. The anomalous Portuguese version, particularly, where Dom João hears lovely singing and sees a girl combing her hair at a pond (Braga, *Romanceiro geral,* p. 26), resembles the scene with the *korrigan* in La Villemarqué's version of the Breton *Aotrou Nann.* In fact the beginning of *La infantina,* if grafted on *La muerte ocultada,* would produce a hybrid very close to the Breton poem. But there Count Nann recognized the woman immediately as a fairy, and her revenge was in keeping with her supernatural character. Sooner or later such nonhuman beings will reveal their origins. In a Basque tale, compared by Caro Baroja to *La infantina encantada,* a *lamiña* (mythological nonhuman female) dressed in gold proposes marriage to a shepherd who, like the knight in the *romance,* goes to ask his mother. On his return he finds the *lamiña* combing her hair, but—unlike the knight in the *romance*—he notices that she has the feet of a goose. Also unlike the outcome of the *romance,* though in keeping with the usual vengeful reaction of a rejected fairy, is his subsequent illness and death.[61] In the *romance,* the only punishment is the disappointment and self-inflicted suffering of the knight. Also the successful departure of the infanta (in some versions with her father) points toward her human nature. It would further be very irregular for a fairy to pretend she has been enchanted by fairies. While it is possible that the *infantina* was a human, changed by fairies temporarily into one of their own kind (see chap. 5 regarding the *xanas* of Asturias), any knight in the ballad world would have known that such a pseudo-fairy could regain her humanness through disenchantment, which he would attempt to accomplish.

To sit in trees is nothing unusual for ballad ladies, whether bewitched or not. Sir Lionel (Child 18) finds on a hunting trip the lady of a slain knight in a tree: "And as he rode still on the plaine/He saw a lady sitt in a graine." In a Greek prose tale, mixed with a few verses, a prince falls in love with a princess who is sitting in a tree; an old woman coaxes her down by sifting flour through a reversed sieve (*Deutsche Volkslieder,* 4:144). The monster in *Kemp Owyne* (Child 34 A) is not sitting in a tree, but her long hair is "twisted thrice about the tree."

Since disenchantment—even disenchantment by love—is usually the result of an act of courage, a man sometimes loses his chance because his courage fails him. In a Scottish tradition, the unearthly sounds of the fairy cavalcade at Halloween kept a farmer from retrieving his wife (Child, 1:336). In another tradition, a queen who has been turned into a huge toad can be disenchanted by a man who arrives on the one Christmas Eve in seven when the cave is open and performs several feats that climax in kissing the toad three times; but all who have tried have either fallen into a trance or lost their courage (Child, 1:311). According to a Portuguese tradition, which has given rise to the *Moira Encantada,* a beautiful girl appears on the Eve of Saint John, at midnight, in the Moorish castle of Tavira and begs to be disenchanted. In the *romance*, Dom Ramiro fails to gain her because the ascent of the wall is too difficult and the hour of disenchantment is up before he reaches the summit (Braga, *Romanceiro geral,* p. 107).

But most ballads have a hero who overcomes such obstacles. How seeming animals are returned to their human shape by bloody sacrifice or a kiss was described earlier. Often a beautiful girl has been changed into a hideous hag, but Kemp Owyne (Child 34) is brave enough to give such a monster the three saving kisses; Sir Gawain (Child 31) is willing to marry one; King Henry (Child 32) slays his steed, his hounds, and his hawks to feed the "grisly ghost," and finally lets her bed down with him. These three knights carry away the prize—the beautiful lady they have unspelled. In his discussions of the three ballads, Child lists a large number of tales and medieval romances and an Icelandic saga of similar content, concluding that "tales resembling the Marriage of Gawain must have been widely spread during the Middle Ages" (1:292). Similarly, in the Irish legend of *The Enchanted Fawn* Lugaid Laigde volunteers when a loathly hag demands that one of the young knights sleep with her; she turns into a beautiful woman and tells him she is the Kingship of Alba (Scotland) and Erin.[62]

The perplexing feature in *La infantina* is that the girl already is as beautiful as any knight may wish. In this case it would be natural for her to be surrounded by unsurmountable difficulties, as in the *Moira Encantada,* above, or by dangers such as the bear and the lion who have guarded a lady for many years but submit to the courageous Young Svendal in a Danish ballad.[63] In short, a knight normally performs an act of courage and gets his lady. Of the knight in *La infantina* no such act is required; he could have the lovely girl on his own terms. The reason for the knight's vacillation remains unexplained; there is only room for some conjectures. Perhaps he lacked the qualifications that are listed in the introductory stanza of *King Henry* (Child 32)—the story of a man who succeeds on every count where the knight in the *romance* fails:

> Lat never a man a wooing wend
> That lacketh thingis three;
> A routh of gold, an open heart,
> Ay fu o charity.

A comparison with King Henry clarifies, at least, the function of the introductory hunt motif in *La infantina*. Before King Henry is visited by the monster whom he proceeds to unspell, he triumphs as a hunter:

> He chas'd the deer now him before,
> An the roe down by the den.
> Till the fattest buck in a' the flock
> King Henry he has slain.

Also Lugaid Laigde and his brothers have just caught their father's enchanted fawn and eaten it when the future bride enters in the shape of a hideous hag. A successful hunt heralds in these poems the successful disenchantment of a lady. This, in turn, tends to undercut the hypothesis of Daniel Devoto, in his discussion of *La infantina* and other ballads, that the hunter who finds a girl has been preoccupied with, or disposed toward, a girl—in violation of a primitive hunting taboo—and, therefore, cannot catch any game (p. 490). Throughout the present chapter, there is ample evidence that success in hunting, or lack of it, is hardly the principal theme of these predominantly anthropocentric Western ballads. Rather, the introductory motif of the unlucky hunt is, among other things, a symbolic paraphrase of the story that follows, as it was in the *romances* that dealt with death. Fortune has turned her back on the hunter; he loses his falcon, wears out his dogs and himself, and analogously, loses his chance to win a lady. Thus, there is no discrepancy between the function of the hunt motif in this *romance* and in the others discussed earlier. The futile hunt is the beginning of the disintegration of the knight.

If, however, the hunting scene were only an allegorical summary of the subsequent narrative, it is doubtful that it could have become and stayed as popular as it has. To people such as those of northern Spain, where the hunt motif has been fostered, the mystery of a dark forest is a part of actual experience. While there is noticeable avoidance of the explicit mention of supernatural occurrences, the suggestive elements of the hunting scene, which create a supernatural atmosphere, are freely elaborated. In some composite *romances* from Asturias and Santander, the introductory hunt and the description of the girl, taken from *La infantina*, stop short before the motif of the seven-year enchantment, and change into the sportive *Caballero burlado*—not alien to the original outcome, since here, too, the knight misses his chance (believing the girl's story of being the child of lepers, or frightened off by some other deterrent).[64] Even though the plot does not exceed rational boundaries, the details of the initial scene are retained. Instead of the lion and lioness who sing to each other in the Sephardic *Infantina*, a variant of *El caballero burlado* has verses about singing snakes, typical of Asturian *romances*: "Donde canta la culebra, responde la serpentina."[65] A version from Catalonia that omits the girl's declaration of being enchanted, contains, nevertheless, her offer to become the knight's wife, mistress, or servant, as well a the ominous hunt and the resplendent forest:

> No trova perdíu ni dayna   ni cassa morta ni viva.
> Passa per una arboleda   que tota l' en relujía.[66]

While the frequency of the hunt motif as a knight's pastime and as a reason for a man's absence from home has declined, the introductory motif of the lonely, futile hunt has evidently not only survived but gained popularity. It is used even in ballads that do not fully warrant the creation of an ominous atmosphere. *La esposa de don García* is a case in point. It is not a tragic *romance*: the husband whose wife has been abducted by the Moors retrieves her unscathed. That the husband should be hunting when the abductors arrive is an international commonplace, as was shown earlier. But the singers of the *romance* have enlarged the simple explanation of the husband's absence into a sinister hunting scene that culminates in his receiving the ill news—in one variant from a bird:

> A cazar iba, a cazar,   el infante don García;
> a cazar iba, a cazar   por unas sierras arriba,
> donde cae la nieve a copos,   donde cae el agua fría,
> donde nace la culebra,   la sierpe la respondía.
> Llególe la oscura noche   en una triste montiña.
> Arrimóse a un duro tronco,   al más gordo que allí había,
> y en la ramita más alta   un ave así le decía:
> —Vuélvase el conde a su casa,   el infante don García,
> porque a su esposa la llevan   moros por sierras arriba.
>
> (Cossío and Maza, 1:41)

In this particular function, the Spanish motif has a Scottish parallel in *Little Musgrave and Lady Barnard* (Child 81 G), where Lord Barnard has gone "to hunt the fallow deer" and is found in the dark wood by the page who comes to inform him of his wife's infidelity:

> And whan he to the green wood cam,
> 'Twas dark as dark could bee,
> And he fand his maister and his men
> Asleep aneth a tree.

The dismal hunt heads also such unlikely *romances* as *El incrédulo*:

> Jesucristo fue a cazar,   a cazar como solía,
> los perros iban cansados   de subir cuestas arriba.
> Encontróse con un hombre   lleno de melancolía.[67]

The man turns out to be an atheist and is punished in hell. Other variants begin with "El rey Jorge fue a cazar" or "San Matías fue de caza"—characters who seem to have no further bearing on the story, after they have questioned the unbeliever as to the existence of God. In another *romance* on a religious theme, *El posadero de Cristo,* a hunter finds on the street a man in need of help:

> Un cazador iba a caza,   no caza como solía,
> se bajó una calle abajo,   se subío una calle arriba,
> y en el medio de la calle   un pobre sangrando había.[68]

He lodges the poor man—Christ—in his house and receives, as a reward for his charity, chairs in heaven for himself and his whole family. The hunter in this *romance* is most likely a late addition, since he is somewhat out of place walking up and down the street; moreover, in most variants the hospitable man is a farmer on his way to or from his fields.

What has been done in the *Romancero* is not a logical but an intuitive grafting of the motif. The enchanted atmosphere of the forest is transplanted into divers other *romances* where an amazing, marvelous, or supernatural event is about to occur. The initial hunt, whether carried out by the person to whom the extraordinary things happen, the person who makes them happen, or a secondary character, is a key to the mode of the *romance* or of a portion of it. The ties to predictable everyday routine are severed; the man in the ballad and the audience cross the threshold to an imaginary world.

Because of its ubiquity, the introductory motif of the lonely hunter can be called a commonplace, but there are several indications that, even as a commonplace, it has not become meaningless. Since the components of the motif can be found, singly or in larger numbers, in ballads that have a similar story but employ different diction, the transfer of the motif is not merely mechanical. The diction within the motif itself varies from one *romance* to another, yet expresses the same feeling. And in none of the *romances* can the futile hunt be called absurd, even it if lacks a logical connection.

That the hunt as such, independent of the motif in question, evokes the supernatural and marvelous, becomes evident in some other ballads. In an Argentine *romance* the hunter is dissuaded by his lady from exposing himself to the evil powers that lurk in the night:

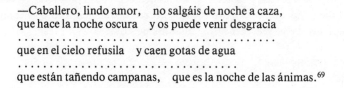

> —Caballero, lindo amor,   no salgáis de noche a caza,
> que hace la noche oscura   y os puede venir desgracia
> ·
> que en el cielo refusila   y caen gotas de agua
> ·
> que están tañendo campanas,   que es la noche de las ánimas.[69]

A lonely hunter may also meet the Serrana—a dangerous woman who dwells in the mountains and whose invitation has led many a man to his death:

> Vio venir un cazador   sin caminos y sin sendas:
> —¡Venga, venga el cazador!   Venga usted para mi cueva;
> será usted bien recibido   y tendrá usted rica cena.[70]

The aggressive huntress, who wears mannish clothes and braids her hair tightly around her head, is thought by Caro Baroja to be the last avatar of an ancient deity of the mountains,[71] hence again a supernatural element in the hunting scene.

As Count Arnaldos is hunting on the morning of Saint John's Day, he falls under the spell of a sailor's song:

> ¡Quién hubiese tal ventura sobre las aguas de mar
> como hubo el conde Arnaldos   la mañana de San Juan!
> Con un falcón en la mano   la caza iba cazar,
> vio venir una galera   que a tierra quiere llegar.
>
> (*Prim.* 153)

Even though the count's adventure is not sylvan but maritime, the hunt is far from being an extraneous element. In the conglomeration of motifs in this ballad that suggest the supernatural, the hunt serves as a complement and reinforcement.

While in the ballads of other countries a great many marvelous things happen during a hunt—elves cast a spell over the hunter, fairy beasts lure him to a hopeless chase, enchanted animals seek restoration to human shape—none has developed of the hunt a lyric motif comparable to that in the *Romancero*. W. M. Hart observes that the popular ballad, in contrast to the "poem of art," does not give special treatment to ghosts or supernatural beings and that "in consequence of this, the supernatural element readily disappears from the ballads, and versions are to be found which contain details only to be understood by comparisons with more original forms."[72] From the *Romancero,* some such beings as Huerco have faded, but their function is compensated, restored, and replenished by the hunt that suggests the presence of supernatural powers.

3

MEASURE AND MOCK-UP

Games

A game is inherently a surrogate or a symbol. In its well-delimited microcosm, a game candidly spells out an order that, in fact, governs human life at large but is often obscured by its complexities. Symbolism and substitution being, thus, their very nature, games have an obvious affinity to poetic diction. Moreover, since the diction of popular ballads well-nigh requires symbols that simultaneously further the narrative, the actual practice of games in a given period makes them especially suitable for the genre here under discussion. And finally, since action, conflict, and crisis are the stuff of both ballads and games, they form a natural association.

At the same time, the role of games within the daily routine reduces them in some ballads to a low-keyed usefulness in setting the scene or providing an occasion for dramatic action. In particular, the feudal knights' peacetime activities included a large component of games, comparable to that of the hunt, as analyzed in the previous chapter. But, like the hunt, games will be found to have a large variety of functions, ranging from a conventional backdrop to high-powered symbolism.

Knightly games are an indication of the medieval source of many Spanish, Danish, British and—in a different form—Russian ballads. In a ballad that circulated among the nobility, jousting may be the main and only action, revealing the courage, magnanimity, and sense of honor of the characters, as in a Danish ballad based on the Wilkina Saga (DgF 7). However, not only tournament games, but also chess, and particularly often the game of tables—a type of backgammon—mark the ballads that take place on the feudal scene.[1] Epic songs and ballads that deal with Charlemagne's court almost make a commonplace of homicide committed by throwing the enormous chessmen or the heavy board at an adversary:

> Don Tomillas que esto oyera,   con muy gran riguridad
> levantava la su mano,   un bofetón le fue a dar.
> Montesinos con el brazo   el golpe le fue a tomar,
> y echó mano al tablero,   y a don Tomillas fue a dar

un tal golpe en la cabeza   que le hubo de matar.

(*Prim*. 176)

The practice of the game of tables and a considerable number of other games mentioned in ballads is verified in Wace's *Brut,* as summarized by Holmes: "The knights are playing at the targets, showing off their horses, fencing, throwing stones, hurling darts, and wrestling. Ladies watch from the walls. Some are playing at chess, others at dice. These gamesters sit two at a table, and the gamesters are constantly borrowing from those who stand by, allowing twelve deniers in repayment for eleven received. Some are taking off pieces of clothing for wagers, and some of the players are almost stripped."[2]

In Spanish *romances*, the gambling on a board (*tablero*) often occurs together with the tournament game of knocking down a scaffolding (*tablado*)—a pairing that has given rise to interesting mutations in some successive *romances*, which reflect changes on the social scene. The two games were current in the same period and are well distinguished from each other in the *romances* of the cycle of the *Infantes de Salas*:

Doña Lambra con fantasía   grandes tablados armara.
Allí salió un caballero   de los de Córdoba la llana,
caballero en un caballo,   y en su mano una vara;
arremete su caballo,   al tablado la tirara,
. . . .
Oídolo ha un caballero   que es ayo de los infantes.
Llorando de los sus ojos   con gran angustia y pesar,
se fue para los palacios   do los infantes estaban:
unos juegan a los dados,   otros las tablas jugaban.[3]

In later *romances*, the use of the word *tablas* for both games has contributed to a certain vagueness. An example of the period of transition is a variant of *Las señas del esposo,* which uses the term *tablas* alternately for two types of games:

—Mi marido es blanco y mozo,   gentil-hombre y bien cortés,
muy gran jugador de *tablas*   y aun también del ajedrez.
En el pomo de su espada   armas trae de un marqués,
y un ropón de brocado,   y de carmesí el corvés:
cabo el fierro de la lanza   trae un pendón portugués,
que lo ganó a las *tablas*   a un buen conde francés.
—Por esas señas, señora,   su marido muerto es:

> en Valencia le mataron   en casa de un ginovés;
> sobre el juego de las *tablas*   lo matara un milanés;
> muchas damas lo lloraban,   caballeros y un marqués.
> Sobre todos lo lloraba   la hija del ginovés:
> todos dicen a una voz   que su enamorada es.
> (Menéndez y Pelayo, 9:238-39; italics mine)

Since the first mention of *tablas* is followed by chess, the table game is evidently meant. The second *tablas* is more likely a tournament game, because the gentleman won in it a pennant from a count. Another variant of this *romance* eliminates any remaining ambiguity: "Que ganó en unas justas/a un valiente francés" (*Prim.* 156). The third instance, however, refers without any doubt to gambling. Besides joining the two different games of the same name, *Las señas del esposo* exemplifies also the gradual change in customs and the gamut of associations evoked by the mention of each game. The shift in this ballad is at least as revealing as that noted by Menéndez Pidal (*Romancero hispánico*, 1:204) in the epic song and the *romances* about the Infantes de Salas: the lament of the father for his sons omits in the *romance* many of their knightly kills, among others that of the *tablado. Las señas del esposo,* which already in the versions of the sixteenth century makes more of the gambling than of the tourney, tends to leave out in the modern tradition the game of tables altogether and to substitute other games that correspond to the actual customs of the period and the place. Thus, in a version from Soria, the husband is a gambler with dice:

> Mi marido es gentilhombre,   gentilhombre aragonés,
> es jugador a los dados   y entre las damas cortés.
> (Schindler, texts, p. 58)

In a Sephardic variant, the husband supposedly has met with violent death while throwing dice with a Genoan. Also some Chilean variants mention "en el juego de los dados" and "en una mesa vedada" as the occasion of death. The Latin American variant that contains the verses "sobre el juego de las tablas/lo matara un milanés" is spotlighted by Menéndez Pidal as a remarkable case of preservation of a *romance viejo.* He notes also another mutation that reflects a change in customs: the lines "en la plaza de los turcos,/muerto por un genovés" in variants from Lima and Mendoza must have their origin in an older version, "en la mesa de los trucos"—a game now fallen into disuse. It follows naturally that the game is discarded entirely when a different motif is felt to be truer to life, as in Cuba: "Pues lo mataron de un tiro/a la puerta de un café."[4]

There is no need to doubt that the husband in *Las señas del esposo* indeed engaged in games. If, however, the verses about various games were merely a record of the popular pastimes of each period, it is doubtful that they would have survived in the *romance*. In keeping with the concision of the language of this genre, each mention of a game has an essential function. The "identifying description" that the wife gives of her absent husband is an idealized portrait of a gentleman. The fine clothes and, in some variants, blond hair establish his handsomeness; his skill in games elaborates the same theme. Although the terms are specific, as is the rule in ballads, they hardly would add up to the best possible, or even a usable, identification, if this were the true function of the wife's speech. What she really says could be translated into prose in general terms like these: "My husband is young and very handsome. I admire him; there is nobody like him in my eyes. His knightly accomplishments and social graces are bound to make him the center of attention, but they also make him vulnerable. I miss him, and I am worried about him." In short, the description does not identify; instead, it divulges the wife's feelings toward her husband. After this, the disclosure of the supposed death of the husband and the wife's trusting acceptance of the news come as a natural sequence.

The game motif in this ballad offers an excellent example of the economy of ballad language. The same skill that in the wife's admiring description of her husband contributed to the idealization, acquires in the messenger's account of his death somewhat unsavory properties. To excel in a game is one thing, but to be killed in a fight at gambling is another. The defamation of the husband, intended to put the wife's loyalty to a test, is aggravated by the remark that the daughter of the Genoan in whose house the gambling took place was the husband's paramour. When the wife resolutely rejects the advances of the messenger, notwithstanding the news of the inglorious demise of her husband, no further proof of her love and faithfulness is necessary.

Both of the contrasting aspects of the skill at games have parallels in other ballads. It goes without saying that physical excellence always enhances a man's image. Thus, in a Danish ballad, the foundling Axelwold gives an indication of noble blood by surpassing all others in games of strength and skill:

> The King's men went to try their skill
> At pitching bar and stone,
> But forward stepp'd young Axelwold
> And beat them every one.
> (DgF 293, trans. Prior, 3:324)

The Scottish Tam Lin (Child 39 M) distinguishes himself in a ball game:

> There was four-and-twenty earthly boys,
> Wha all played at the ba,
> But Tamas was the bonniest boy,
> And playd the best amang them a'.

A simple enumeration of games in which the hero excelled helps make the lament for the Bonny Earl of Murray (Child 181) one of the most impressive portraits of an ideal knight:

> He was a braw gallant
> And he rid at the ring;
> And the bonny Earl of Murray,
> Oh he might have been a King!
>
> He was a braw gallant
> And he played at the ba;
> And the bonny Earl of Murray
> Was the flower amang them a'.
>
> He was a braw gallant
> And he playd at the glove;
> And the bonny Earl of Murray,
> Oh he was the Queen's love.

In the case of the game of tables, however, only the context can make it clear whether a game has a positive or a negative connotation. The game in itself did not call for reproach. That proficiency in playing tables was as much expected of a knight as jousting is evident in the following two *romances*. In *Crianza de Fernán González,* the charcoal maker who rears the hero teaches him both skills:

No le muestra a cortar leña,   ni menos açer carbón;
muéstrale a jugar las cañas   y mué[s] trale justador,
también a jugar los dados   y las tablas muy mejor.
(*Romancero tradicional,* 2:283)

Likewise, in *Conde Claros de Montalván,* the emperor regards participation in gambling as well as in tournaments as a basic necessity of the count and arranges for a suitable stipend:

—Llámenme mi camarero   de mi cámara real;
dad mil marcos de oro al conde   para sus armas quitar;
dad mil marcos de oro al conde   para mantener verdad;
dalde otros tantos al conde   para vestir y calzar;
dalde otros tantos al conde   para las tablas jugar;
dalde otros tantos al conde   para torneos armar;
dalde otros tantos al conde   para con damas folgar.
(*Prim.* 191)

While the *romance* in which the dead Infantes de Salas are eulogized by their father has lost many of the knightly attributes found in the epic song, there remains in the praise of the second son, Martín Gómez, the distinction in the table game:

Jugador era de tablas   el mejor de toda España,
mesurado caballero,   muy buen hablador en plaza.
(*Prim.* 24)

At the same time, the game of tables can lead to reproach when a knight's addiction to it makes him forget his other duties. In one of the *romances* of Gaiferos (*Prim.* 173), the emperor finds his son-in-law enjoying a game when he should be rescuing his wife from the Moors:

Asentado está Gaiferos   en el palacio real,
asentado al tablero   para las tablas jugar.
Los dados tiene en la mano,   que los quiere arrojar,
cuando entró por la sala   don Carlos el emperante.
Desque así jugar lo vido   empezóle de mirar;
hablándole está hablando   palabras de gran pesar:
—Si así fuésedes, Gaiferos,   para las armas tomar,
como sois para los dados,   y para las tablas jugar,
vuestra esposa tienen moros,   iríadesla a buscar:
pésame a mí por ello   por que es mi hija carnal.[5]

When an honorable death is contrasted to a dishonorable one, the latter is sometimes defined by gambling. Doña Urraca weeps over the death of young Fernán d'Arias, but his father consoles her, pointing out that he died in a noble combat, not in the taverns or playing tables:

> No murió por las tabernas, ni a las tablas jugando;
> mas murió sobre Zamora vuestra honra resguardando.
>
> (*Prim.* 50)

Very similar in its moral attitude is a version of *Conde Claros,* which mentions dice as a possible cause of dishonorable death:

> Quien a mí bien me quisiere, no cure de me llorar,
> que no muero por traidor nin por los dados jugar;
> muero yo por mi señora, que no me puede penar,
> pues el yerro que yo fice no fue mucho de culpar.
>
> (Menéndez y Pelayo, 9:251)

The list of crimes for which the Portuguese libertine Joãosinho is outlawed by his father begins with gambling at Christmas:

> Joãosinho foi jogar uma noite de Natal,
> ganhou cem dobras d'ouro, marcadas e por marcar.
> Matou um padre de missa revestido no altar!
> Enganou sete donzellas que estavam para casar;
> e furtou sete castillos todos do passo real.
>
> (Braga, *Açoriano,* p. 230)

A card game even becomes the occasion for homicide in a Piedmontese ballad, *Mal ferito* (Nigra, p 170): words lead to knives, knives to pistols. The *Rantin Laddie* (Child 240 A) lets games stand as a concrete example of levity of the dishonored girl:

> Aften hae I playd at the cards and the dice,
>   For the love of a bonie rantin laddie,
> But now I maun sit in my father's kitchen-neuk
>   And balow a bastard babie.

Likewise the Breton Fantik Pikart, taken to the scaffold for infanticide, confesses publicly that she went to the manor instead of Mass and met with the young lords over dice and cards.[6]

While the game of tables used to have in the *Romancero* both a derogatory and a laudatory function, the card games often found in *romances* of the modern tradition carry a conspicuously negative meaning. Card playing appears to be equivalent to a testimony of bad character, as in the case of the scoundrel in *La doncella vengadora,* who leaves his card game to pursue a girl:

> La veía un caballero   traidor que la pretendía;
> jugando estaba a los naipes   con el príncipe de Hungría.
> Dejó de jugar los naipes   y fuese a alcanzar la niña.
>   (Cossío and Maza, 1:324)

In another modern *romance*, don Juan is playing with his companions, when a vile woman tells him his wife and children plan to poison him. He goes home and slays them, and then returns to the game as if nothing had happened (Cossío and Maza, 1:398). Callousness is implied by a card game also in *El rapto*:

> De todo lo sucedido   tus padres no saben nada,
> ni tampoco tus hermanos   que con tus nobles criadas
> están jugando a los naipes   y de ti no se acordaban.[7]

As may be expected, Spanish fairy tales coincide with the *romances* in showing by means of gambling a flaw in the character of the hero. For example, a prince unwittingly gambles away his life and soul to the devil— a device characteristic of the Hispanic versions of this tale and infrequent in the rest of Europe, as Espinosa observes.[8]

When games form a prominent episode or the central action of a ballad, they cannot help but retain the two contrasting aspects that became evident in the auxiliary motifs—one marking the hero and the other marking the villain, or, occasionally, the fool.

Card games, especially, lend themselves to comic incidents, unlikely to bring honor. Thus, the gambler in the Piedmontese *Galante spogliato* loses his gold and silver and his clothes to a girl with whom he plays cards in the shade of a mulberry tree. The judge lets the girl keep her spoils, and the man cannot even hide his disgrace from his mother, who sees him arrive barefoot and in shirtsleeves.[9]

In contrast, skill in knightly games is not only an enhancing attribute of a hero, but winning a game functions also as a favorable omen. Triumph at a tourney foretells triumph in a crucial situation. Guarinos, who has been languishing seven years in a Moorish dungeon, receives permission

on Saint John's Day to participate in the contest of knocking down a
tablado, which has proved too much for the Moors. Although Guarinos's
arms have rusted and his horse has been carrying lime for seven years, he
strikes down more than half of the scaffolding:

> Marlotes desque lo vido   con reir y con burlar
> dice que vaya al tablado   y lo quiera derribar.
> Guarinos con grande furia   un encuentro le fue a dar,
> que más de la mitad dél   en el suelo fue a echar.
> > (*Prim.* 186)

The game in this *romance* is an excellent example of a narrative device
serving a multiple purpose: characterization, foreshadowing, prolonging
the pleasurable part of the plot, and facilitation of the visual expression of
the theme. Since superiority in a tournament customarily gives a knight the
credentials of a hero, Guarinos's stature is established by his feat at the
tablado. Since the ballad brings the contest before the audience, the game
can also prepare for a subsequent, more vital triumph of the hero. Instead
of letting Guarinos overwhelm his guards and escape, the ballad gives the
listeners double pleasure by enacting the victory first in a game and then in
a struggle for life or death. At the same time, the preparatory game conforms more closely than the final combat itself to the usage of the
Romancero, since its fewer participants allow greater visual clarity than
the ensuing melee. In the *romance* in question, the circumstances of the
tournament are presented in leisurely fashion, to be savored one by one,
while the skirmish with the Moors, even though Guarinos gains in it life
and liberty, is reported in a few lines. After he carries away the victory in
the tournament, it appears to be a foregone conclusion that he will accomplish also the much more prodigious feat of vanquishing single-handed the
innumerable Moors who attack him. Thus, the spotlight is turned from the
real-life happenings to a stylized paraphrase of these happenings without
any diminution of the heroic mode of the poem.

A similar shift of emphasis occurs in the British *Hugh Spencer's Feats in
France* (Child 158). The ballad tells in detail how Hugh finds the French
horses unfit, rides his own old hackney, and defeats the French champion.
As in the *romance* about Guarinos, fewer verses are devoted here to the decisive action, although the latter is of immeasurably greater magnitude:
still threatened with beheading, Hugh kills a large number of the men of
King Charles of France, whereupon Charles offers peace to the English
king.

Whereas the structure of the stories of Guarinos and Hugh Spencer retains a clearly discernible line of demarcation between game and real conflict, some Russian *byliny,* such as *Stavr Godinovich* (Trautmann, pp. 191-92), fuse them into one, typically elaborating the game into a kind of triathlon. In order to free her captive husband, Stavr's wife dresses as a messenger from the Golden Horde and goes to Prince Vladimir of Kiev, demanding tribute for twelve years. When Vladimir requires her to compete with the champions of Kiev, she wins the wrestling match, beheading one opponent, smashing the ribs of another and the brains of the third, all of which causes the rest to flee. Then, she proceeds to win a sharpshooting contest, and finally three chess games against Prince Vladimir. The outcome of the games is sufficient to lead Vladimir to surrender to the invincible stranger. In another *bylina* (Trautmann, pp. 274-78), Dobrynya and Vasily Kazimirov extract tribute from Czar Batur by defeating him at cards and dice, scoring highest at sharpshooting, and winning a wrestling match with the czar's Tatars. The combinations in the Russian tests are, thus, manifold: sport is mixed with carnage; physical superiority, with the mental acuteness of chessplaying and with the favor of fortune in games of chance. It must be noted that here gambling is not a weakness or a vice, but one of the many skills of the champion.

In one respect closely related to the foregoing, but in another linked to the function of games as courtship are the ballads about the knight who wins a lady by proving his physical skills in a public exhibition. In *Toros y cañas* (Cossío and Maza, 2:32), don Pedro Salazar gains the hand of the lovely doña Juana by killing a huge bull of Jarama before king and court. Similarly, in the British *Will Stewart and John* (Child 107), the Earl of Mar's daughter promises to love Will if he wins the "greater part" of sixteen ball games. Also in *Lord Livingston* (Child 262), a game is expected by the competing lords to earn for the winner the favor of a lady. The gallant aspect of competing for a lady in a public pageant is forfeited, however, when a woman is an unwilling wager in a game such as chess. According to Armistead and Silverman, the latter device "is characteristic of the Judeo-Spanish versions [of *Rico Franco*] from the Eastern Mediterranean, in contrast to the sixteenth-century texts and Portuguese and Catalan versions, in which she is abducted."[10] The sordidness of the affair is intensified by the winner's jeering account of the fate of the girl's family: he has turned her parents into jailer and cook and has killed all three of her brothers (Menéndez y Pelayo, 10:323). The Sephardic *Jugador* bestows some glory on the winner, but mainly shame on the one who gambled away his wife:

> Ganárame mi caballo,   mi caballo, y mi bordón,
> ganárame el mi anillo,   mi anillo y mi reloj,
> ganárame mi esposica,   ¡mi alma y mi corazón!
> Después que la hubo ganado,   cabe mí me la besó.
> Vámonos a preguntarla   a quién quería mejor.
> —Mejor quiero al que me gana   que al traidor que me jugó.[11]

The game never comes off, though its purpose is fulfilled, in a version of the Piedmontese *Ritorno del soldato*. Margherita's first sweetheart arrives, after seven years in the war, on her wedding day. He proposes a card game with the bride as a stake, but when he reveals his identity, Margherita immediately declares herself for him, her "prim amante."[12] Here the card game casts no undesirable reflection upon the man who suggests it, since the context indicates that the decision actually rests with Margherita and not with the cards.

In a slightly different way, the formal conflict of a game accompanies the vital conflict between the characters in the Danish *Unge Hr. Tor og Jomfru Tore* (DgF 72). Like the returning soldier in the Piedmontese ballad, who challenged his sweetheart to a decision, Sir Tor wins back Lady Tore, about to marry another, during a chess game with the lady herself. In his comments on this ballad, Prior (3:151) remarks that "descriptions of chess combats occur frequently in old romances" and that "our hero arriving by sea with his chess-board and entering the hall to challenge the guests is just what we find in Sir Tristrem Fytte I, st. 28." Nevertheless, the games played by Tor and Tore are not a meaningless commonplace. He wins the first game and taunts her for her faithlessness; she wins the second game and justifies herself. Thus, attack and defense are expressed simultaneously in words and game, the latter making the dialogue more forceful.

Games function as courtship—implied in several ballads already discussed—also in the Danish *Taerningspillet* (DgF 238): in a table game with a horseboy, a girl wagers, and loses, her honor and her troth; fortunately for her, the horseboy turns out to be a prince. Many Danish ballads show chess and other table games as a customary, perhaps even compulsory, feature in courtship, with the obvious symbolism of "winning" a bride (DgF 40, 75, 477). A highly formal occasion is described in *Dronning Dagmar og Junker Strange* (DgF 132), where Strange, sent by the king to fetch his bride, wins three games against Dagmar before claiming her for the king. This poem draws from Prior (2:125) the following comment: "This playing of chess with a young lady occurs so frequently, that we may infer from it that a knowledge of the game was considered a great accomplishment in a maiden, and is mentioned as implying that she was well bred. It is singular that it is at the time of betrothal that it is most usually played, perhaps as a test of her temper, but possibly to give that kind of claim to her that winning a stake conveys." Also a rather recent Russian ballad, *The King of Sweden and Yekaterina Alekseyevna*, contains a letter sent by the Russian empress in answer to the Swedish king's threat that he will marry Yekaterina to his son: "According to our custom, first one stays as a guest, then one marries. Come as a guest to the Czarina, come to look me over. I will play with you cards and checkers" (Trautmann, p. 422). This invitation to courtship, however, lures the Swedes into a lethal trap set by the Russians. In another *bylina,* the nominal stake is a hundred rubles, but after losing three chess games to Churilo Plenkovich, Katerina confesses she has fallen hopelessly in love with him (Trautmann, p. 351).

The reason for such a lengthy discussion of courtship by a table game as shown in non-Hispanic ballads is that its infrequence in the *Romancero* might otherwise impede proper identification. It does occur in the *Romance primero de Moriana*:

> Moriana en un castillo   juega con el moro Galván;
> juegan los dos a las tablas   por mayor placer tomar.
> Cada vez que el moro pierde   bien perdía una cibdad;
> cuando Moriana pierde   la mano le da a besar.[13]

Galván, though having Moriana in his power, sensuously prolongs his pleasure by courting her over a game of tables. The implications of this game for Galván are restated more explicitly in the *Romance tercero de Moriana* (*Prim.* 123). Here, the Moor addresses his former captive, who is now safe in her husband's castle:

> De aquel buen tiempo pasado   te debrías recordar
> cuando dentro en mi castillo   conmigo solías folgar:
> cuando contigo jugaba   mi alma debrías mirar
> cuando ganaba perdiendo,   porque era el perder ganar:

cuando merescí ganando   tus bellas manos besar,
y más cuando en tu regazo   me solía reclinar,
y cuando con tí fablando   durmiendo solía quedar.
Si esto non fue amor, señora,   ¿cómo se podrá llamar?

Moriana answers that she humored the Moor only to await rescue by her husband. Since this is known also to the audience of the first ballad, the game functions there as a visible expression of the wordless tension and Moriana's secretly defensive attitude. The years of waiting and pretense are condensed into the brief scene of a game of tables—a choice example of reduction of amorphous material into a well-delineated scene, typical of the diction of ballads.

Another case of unwelcome courtship at a table game is that of *Venturilla*:

Moro viejo la vendía,   moro mozo la compraba;
comprábala moro rico,   de rico muy grande fama.
Con él comía y bebía,   con él jugaba a la tabla:
—Dime, Venturilla, dime: ¿Eres soltera o casada?
—Eso qué preguntas, Moro,   ¿por qué me lo preguntabas?
—Lo pregunto, Venturilla,   que has de ser mi namorada.[14]

The Hispanic *romances* tend to differ from other European ballads that show courtship by a table game, in their insinuation of duress. For example, the crudeness of the gambling for the girl in *Rico Franco* is not evident in the Piedmontese *Ritorno del soldato,* which comes closer to the symbolic chess game in some Danish ballads. The villain in *Venturilla,* a *romance* similar to *Rico Franco*, becomes no better by making the prey a participant in the game. On the whole, however, there is a great deal of overlapping in the three foregoing varieties—competing in a game for the favor of a woman, wagering a woman in a gamble, and courting a woman over chess or tables. The difference is in nuance and not in essence; he who wins the game wins the woman. Even the knights who joust with each other to win the favor of a lady and the sordid gamblers who wager a woman compete basically for the same stake.

As a factor in courtship, a game has the dual nature characteristic of most ballad motifs. As a device in ballad diction, it is a visible, condensed, localized expression of the emotional conquest, while there is little doubt that such games also represent the wooing customs of the period.

Besides the two aspects just mentioned, there is a third that reaches beyond the game itself: the element of fate, brought into the ballad by the game, continues to affect the lives of the players. In the *romances* of Moriana, as well as in *Venturilla,* the final outcome is unfavorable to the man, even though the woman was at first the threatened party. The same type of change of fortune occurs in *Venganza de honor* (Cossío and Maza, 1:327, 328), in which Isabel is playing the *juego del alfiler* when her abductor appears. It seems that even this guileless game can unleash demons who then wilfully manipulate the lives of the participants. A game functions as a symbol of a life full of uncontrollable events in the long Danish ballad, *Aslag Tordsøn og skøn Valborg* (DgF 475). Although the child Valborg does not participate in the game of chance played by the ladies of the court, it is she who experiences "a shifting course of luck" throughout an involved story of loving and losing. Thus, even a game that has no logical connection with the plot is not necessarily an extraneous addition. Often the ballad deals with an unexpected turn of events, a shift of fortune, or a reversal of the relative position of two adversaries. The game, though sometimes divorced from the story of the ballad, creates an atmosphere of tension and imminence of change. In short, it puts the listener on guard. Ballads generally do not contain surprises in the true sense of the word; the pleasure of the listener derives, rather than from startling turns, from a gradual preparation by means of advance announcements. A game is one of the motifs that channel his expectations in the direction that the ballad is about to follow.

The use of a game to mark the fate of the persons exemplifies the conventional way ballads have of implying the vast and conceptual through the limited, concrete, and visible. A throw of dice or a move on the chessboard can change the relative standing of the players in the game; at the same time, the game gives a signal for fate to intervene, not only in the game, but also in the lives of all concerned. When Galván plays with Moriana at tables, he challenges fate; Moriana submits to fate. Even though Galván, at the moment, seems to have full power over his captive, it is she whom fate favors in the end.

It follows that the act of abruptly cutting a game short expresses defiance of fate. In a Russian *bylina,* Dobrynya is diverting himself with a game on a golden chessboard, not knowing that his betrothed, Nastasya, is marrying Alyosha, the only man he had forbidden her to marry. When Dobrynya receives the news, he flings his golden board down, so that the earth quakes, and rushes off to stop the wedding.[15] When King Valdemar receives an urgent message from the queen, who is dying in childbed, he tries to race death:

> The King his chequer board shut in haste,
> The dice they rattled and rung;
> "Forbid it our Father who dwells in heaven
> That Dagmar should die so young!"
> (DgF 135, trans. Prior, 2:138)

As the king in the Sephardic *Hijo vengador* (Larrea, 2:87) hears his unborn son predict that he will take the life of both parents, he tosses down the dice he was holding and goes to tell the queen that, if her child is male, he will be given to a lioness:

> Oyéndolo está el buen rey   desde su sala reale;
> dados tenía en la mano   y al suelo los arrojase,
> fuése para los palacios   donde la reina estare.

The same wording is used in another Sephardic *romance, Búcar sobre Valencia* (Larrea, 1:51). The Moor's threat to take Valencia and to enslave the Cid's women causes the Cid to throw down his dice and to begin devising a trap for Búcar:

> Oído lo había el buen Sidi   desde su sala donde estaba,
> los dados tiene en la mano   al suelo los arrojara,
> fuese para los palacios   donde la Urraca estaba.

Gaiferos, being upbraided by his father-in-law for not rescuing his wife (see above), would hurl away the entire gaming table, were it not for the respect he has for his partner:

> Levantóse del tablero   no queriendo más jugar,
> y tomáralo en las manos   para haberlo de arrojar,
> si no por él que con él juega,   que era hombre de linaje:
> jugaba con él Guarinos   almirante de la mar.[16]

Granted that throwing down the chessboard, the dice, or the table board can be simply a sign of impatience and agitation, it is significant that the objects thrown are those employed in games; the violent interruption of a game conveys the determination of the hero to force fate.

None of the categories discussed up to now is fully applicable to *Fajardo* (*Prim.* 83); still, it has subtle affinities to many of the foregoing ballads.

Here the game, together with the accompanying dialogue, takes up the whole *romance*:

> Jugando estaba el rey moro   y aun al ajedrez un día,
> con aquese buen Fajardo   con amor que le tenía.
> Fajardo jugaba a Lorca,   y el rey moro Almería;
> jaque le dio con el roque,   el alférez le prendía.
> A grandes voces dice el moro: —La villa de Lorca es mía.—
> Allí hablara Fajardo,   bien oiréis lo que decía:
> —Calles, calles, señor rey,   no tomes la tal porfía,
> que aunque me la ganases,   ella no se te daría:
> caballeros tengo dentro   que te la defenderían.—
> Allí hablara el rey moro,   bien oiréis lo que decía:
> —No juguemos más, Fajardo,   ni tengamos más porfía,
> que sois tan buen caballero,   que todo el mundo os temía.

A Christian chief and a Moorish king, good friends by all accounts, are playing chess, with towns as stakes. There is, however, a trace of the tension of conquest and defense that pervaded the games played during courtship. And courtship it is, as we find it, in Moorish tradition, which personifies towns as brides. This tradition was continued in *romances* dealing with Moorish subjects. For example, in the *Romance de Abenámar* (*Prim.* 78a) King Juan offers to marry the town of Granada, but the latter answers that she is married to the Moor, who loves her well. In *Fajardo* when the Moorish king claims the town of Lorca as his prize, Fajardo answers as if Lorca were a woman wooed: "She would not give herself to you." Wagering a town resembles here wagering a woman. In the *romances* where a girl was the stake in a game, such as some variants of *Rico Franco,* she retained her own will and imposed it at the end by killing her "owner." This kind of will is attributed in *Fajardo* also to the town of Lorca. At the same time, Fajardo himself is a person of strong will, who refuses to let a mere game affect the reality of the Reconquest; he does not fling down the chessboard in the manner of some other resolute men, but his reply to the Moor counts for as much, so that the latter withdraws from the game.

The minimum of overt action in *Fajardo* did not keep Lope de Vega from recognizing its concentrated dramatic tension and incorporating it into his play *El primer Fajardo.* The Moorish king and Fajardo are on stage, playing chess; the *romance* is sung at the same time by the musicians, until the king exclaims: "You lost, friend Fajardo; the town of

Lorca is mine!'' In the opinion of Menéndez Pidal, this play is the most accomplished example of the fusion of *romance* and drama, customary during that period.[17]

This easy blending of *romance* and theater points to the great similarity between the two genres, and, in particular, to the theatrical presentation of table games in ballads. In the course of a few minutes, the ambitions of the characters and their conflicts with each other can be shown to the eye of the spectator or to the imagination of the listener. The limited number of actors—in most cases only two—allows the scene not only to be enacted easily in the theater, but also to be imagined quickly. The same qualities were obvious in the tournament games that in some ballads displaced real battles. The singer, by his use of games, contracts both time and space, and, at the same time, gives visual concreteness to complex ideas and moods.

To return to one of the initial premises in this chapter: a game, being a microcosm—simpler, clearer, shorter than life, and yet its image—and being a microcosm not coincidentally but essentially, is with the greatest ease translated back into the macrocosm without any conscious, rational, process. For this reason, games in ballads not only enhance or defame character, but also reveal, accentuate, or paraphrase psychological processes, and even crystallize an elusive metaphysical concept—fate—into an almost tangible presence.

4

A Symbol
for All Seasons
Clothing

The extreme poverty of the lingua franca of ballads becomes clearly evident in the use of clothing as a symbol. Makers of ballads have continually reached for it to meet contingencies in poetic expression. This seeming poverty, in turn, has resulted in enormous wealth in the variety of applications. Indeed a complete ballad could be constructed from different references to clothing: characters would be identified, their emotions expressed, their relations with each other explored, their good or ill fortune documented, and judgment passed upon them by their fellowmen—all this, by means of a sole symbol. This chapter will offer some examples of the prodigious versatility of the symbol and, in conclusion, some possible reasons for showing clothing such favoritism.

One of the most striking examples of the complex symbolism of clothing is a Spanish commonplace, used in several *romances* to introduce the protagonist:

> Un rey tenía una hija,   una hija no más tenía,
> de plata la trae calzada,   de oro la trae vestida.
> (Cossío and Maza, 2:161)

The first impression is, perhaps, that of the wealth and splendor of a royal child dressed in silver and gold, but an additional nuance is readily perceptible in another variant of the same ballad, in which the parents are not king and queen: "Que su padre la calzaba   y su madre la vestía." The security enjoyed by the daughter is not only material but also emotional: she is loved, sheltered, and cared for. Hence, also the gold and silver are concise symbols of the conglomerate joys and satisfactions that constitute the best possible life.[1]

While these meanings of clothing may be termed a stylization of the real circumstance, a third application clearly represents poetic substitution:

La hija del rey   la llevan cautiva,
de oro calzada   de plata ceñida.
Dice la reina mora,   qué esclava tan linda,
que entre mis tres hijas   reina parecía.
—Échala a lavar, madre,   a la fuente fría,
que esas sus colores   ya las perdería.
(Cossío and Maza, 1:339)

The transition, within ten hexasyllables, may seem abrupt: the princess is abducted in costly clothing, but the jealous eye of the Moorish girl falls on her complexion. Obviously, a metonymic process is here at work: when a ballad speaks of fine attire, it often means physical beauty—not beauty acquired by means of clothes, but natural beauty that exists and needs to be expressed in images that have been established within the conventions of balladry.

A few examples from other ballads will substantiate this interpretation. The sleepless night Count Claros spends thinking about Claralinda is doubtless due to the beauty of the princess herself, not her dress and shoes, even though her beauty is verbally attributed to her clothing:

Son las doce de la noche,   los gallos quieren cantar,
don Carlos se muere de amores   que ni puede sosegar.
Vio salir a Claralinda   de su palacio real;
era hermosa como el oro   por su vestir y calzar.
(Cossío and Maza, 1:112)

A similar switch occurs at the end of the French-Provençal *Atours de Marie-Madeleine,* when Mary Magdalen, after dressing in seven ells of velvet, winding a sash twenty-four times around her waist, and donning an apron of thirty-six colors, stuns both nature and clergy, but defies the reproachful priest by insisting on her right to her God-given beauty:

"No l'abaisse per persona,   l'abaissarèi pas per vos:
Le bon Dio la m'a donada,   la portarèi tos los jors!"
(Doncieux, p. 170)

In other words, the hyperbolic dressing scene is not so much a manifestation of luxury as a symbol of Mary Magdalen's prodigious natural beauty.

Likewise, in *La Condesita,* the lines about dress and shoes are hardly a realistic statement (especially since the countess who draws her fickle husband's curiosity is dressed as a pilgrim), but, rather, an extension of the first member of the series—"halagüeña en el mirar"—which refers to her natural attractiveness:

> —¿Quién es esta peregrina   halagüeña en el mirar,
> halagüeña en el vestir,   halagüeña en el calzar?[2]

In some variants of this *romance*, the applications of clothing are compounded. The countess, as she sets out to look for her husband, asks her father to dress her in coarse cloth, not in silk or gold. Is her purpose simply to remain unrecognized by "those who have eaten her bread"? Does she expect the lowly habit to make her appearance all the more dazzling when she finally sheds it and reveals the green shift that the count had given her for Christmas? Or does her request approximate the vows of austerity, made in times of unrighted wrongs, such as those of the Marquis of Mantua, "de nunca peinar mis canas   ni las mis barbas cortar;/de no vestir otras ropas,   ni renovar mi calzar"? The variety of questions that arise points to clothing as a typical example of the high condensation of multiple meanings that can be often discovered behind a ballad commonplace or a formula. In one text, the husband gives orders after the happy reunion with his wife:

> —Cogerme esa peregrina,—   subírmela arriba ya,
> vestirla de oro y seda   y llevarla a pasear.
> (*Romancero tradicional*, 4:48)

What is it that is restored to her with clothes of gold and silk? Wealth? Status? Her husband's love? Probably all three, and likewise her beauty, since she again has reason to be beautiful.

Similarly, the girl retrieved from Moorish captivity expresses her impatience to resume all the joys and comforts of her former way of life, when she laments the damage done to her favorite outfit during her absence: "¡Mi jubón de grana,   mi saya querida,/que te dejé nueva   y te hallo rompida!" The mother hastens to reassure her with words that seemingly deal only with a garment but contain the promise of complete restoration of her former station: "Calla, hija, calla,   hija de mi vida;/que quien te echó esa   otra te echaría" (Menéndez y Pelayo, 10:58).

When a noble person has to assume temporarily the identity of a commoner or a peasant, he makes sure of retaining his former attire—and thus his real status—under the disguise. As Charlemagne's son is about to be hanged as an insolent pilgrim, a costly robe comes to light under his tattered cloak:

> Desnúdanle una esclavina   que no valía un reale;
> ya le desnudaban otra   que valía una ciudade;
> halládole han al infante,   halládole han la señale.
> (*Prim.* 195)

While in this *romance* the costly clothes lead to, but do not constitute, the decisive identification, a Russian prince in similar circumstances is saved from beheading by the discovery of a czar's robe and ring under his merchant's gown (Trautmann, p. 435).

In Danish *viser,* a line such as "in robe of sable dressed" or "arrayed in scarlet pall" is synonymous with "noble lord" or "noble lady." Before a person of rank appears among others, he almost invariably is said to draw on his cloak. In the *Romancero* there is little to match this particular Danish formula, except some isolated cases, such as the Sephardic *Infanta deshonrada*:

> Dezíanselo a la reina,   la reina no lo creía.
> Cobijóse en manto de oro,   fue a ver si es verdad o mentira.
> (Larrea, 2:34)

However, the fusion of ceremonial clothes and the office that they represent is strikingly evident in *Prim.* 33, where a threat to the pope's robes is enough to make him acquiesce to the Cid's demands:

> —Si no me absolvéis, el Papa,   seríaos mal contado:
> que de vuestras ricas ropas   cubriré yo mi caballo.
> El Papa, desque lo oyera,   tal respuesta le hubo dado:
> —Yo te absuelvo, don Rodrigo,   yo te absuelvo de buen grado,
> que cuanto hicieres en Cortes   seas de ello libertado.

Even more famous is *Prim.* 52, in which the Cid warns the king of the consequences of perjury—dishonorable death in the hands of peasants—and accentuates the inequality of status, and, thus, the threat, by a description of the killer's lowly clothes:

> —Villanos te maten, Alonso,   villanos, que non hidalgos,
> . . . .
> abarcas traigan calzadas,   que no zapatos con lazo;

> capas traigan aguaderas,   no de contray, ni frisado;
> con camisones de estopa,   no de holanda, ni labrados.

Since here the antithesis results from the dovetailing of a series of the possible with a series of the impossible, and indeed the situation is hypothetical rather than actual, the contrast is visually perhaps not quite so forceful as it usually is in descriptions of persons the balladist wants his public to "see" at the moment. One of the most common purposes of contrasting the clothing of different characters is to identify the hero or heroine among the rest, often by means of a series of verses about secondary characters, followed by a brief but impressive description of the clothing of the main personage. The *Romancero* and the ballads of other countries are alike in highlighting the protagonist by presenting him in distinctive dress; yet the Spanish tend to mention less color, but more gold, silver, precious fabrics, and fine leather, than, for example, the British. The latter often dress the heroine in green; or, when given a choice, she may pick white or scarlet, as does Fair Janet (Child 64):

> Some put on the gay green robes,
> And some put on the brown;
> But Janet put on the scarlet robes,
> To shine foremost throw the town.

The Spanish heroine, on the other hand, is likely to wear, rather than a particular color, a finer fabric than other women:

> Sacan a la una   vestida de lana;
> dice el rey de Francia: —Esta no es mi novia.
> Sacan a la otra   vestida de grana;
> dice el rey de Francia: —Esta no es mi novia.
> Sacan a la chica   vestida de seda,
> dice el rey de Francia: —Esta es mi novia.[3]

One might almost say that the Spanish singers have made a point of avoiding the mention of specific colors, as in *Prim.* 59:

> Ellos en aquesto estando,   el buen Cid que asomó,
> con trescientos caballeros,   todos hijosdalgo son,
> todos vestidos de un paño,   de un paño y una color,
> si no fuera el buen Cid,   que traía un albornoz.

Likewise, doña Alda (*Prim*. 184) is distinguished from her ladies simply as not resembling them:

> En París está doña Alda,   la esposa de don Roldán,
> trescientas damas con ella   para la acompañar:
> todas visten un vestido,   todas calzan un calzar,
> todas comen a una mesa   todas comían de un pan,
> si no era doña Alda,   que era la mayoral.

In both of these *romances*, the hero or heroine stands out from the entourage by different clothes—the Cid's three hundred men are said to be dressed in "the same color"—but what the contrasting colors are, the singer will not tell. These descriptions have the flexibility of stage directions that leave the choice of colors in each production up to the costumer—a freedom needed also by a singer who uses visual aids, as suggested in the last section of this chapter.

In the old heroic *romances* we sometimes find series of antithetical verses that express more than just the identity of the hero. When elegant clothes are placed opposite a suit of armor, the latter implies not only the superiority of the hero as a warrior but also his determination to hold his own. Thus clothing becomes a means of communicating psychological states. The series of parallel antitheses of courtier's clothes and warrior's clothes is typical of the *romances* about early Spanish heroes, such as Fernán González (*Prim*. 16), who, menaced by the king, points out his own fighting strength:

> Vos venís en gruesa mula,   yo en ligero caballo;
> vos traéis sayo de seda,   yo traigo un arnés tranzado;
> vos traéis alfanje de oro,   yo traigo lanza en mi mano;
> vos traéis cetro de rey,   yo un venablo acerado;
> vos con guantes olorosos,   yo con los de acero claro;
> vos con la gorra de fiesta,   yo con un casco afinado;
> vos traéis ciento de mula,   yo trescientos de caballo.

Similar terms are used in *Prim*. 29 to prepare the audience for the Cid's resolution and implacability, as he rides with his father to the king's court:

> Todos cabalgan a mula,   sólo Rodrigo a caballo;
> todos visten oro y seda,   Rodrigo va bien armado;
> todos espadas ceñidas,   Rodrigo estoque dorado;
> todos con sendas varicas,   Rodrigo lanza en la mano;
> todos guantes olorosos,   Rodrigo guante mallado;

todos sombreros muy ricos,   Rodrigo casco afilado,
y encima del casco lleva   un bonete colorado.

In the last two examples, clothing not only identifies the hero and describes his permanent quality as a fighter, but also reveals his attitude in a specific situation. When the hero is unaware of a trap laid for him, his good faith and guilelessness may be demonstrated by his festive clothes, as, for example, the fine shirt, green embroidered jacket, buckskin boots, and gilded spurs of Sir Karl in a Danish ballad (DgF 116) or the gold and brocade of don Fadrique (*Prim.* 65), who starts out for a tournament in Seville, not knowing that his brother, King Pedro, will have him beheaded:

Yo, Maestre sin ventura,   yo, maestre desdichado,
tomara trece de mula,   veinte y cinco de caballo,
todos con cadenas de oro   y jubones de brocado.

Except in specific instances, as the one just cited, Spanish knights stand out with their austerity. Brave Danes may combine a coat of mail with a fine silk shirt, as does Peder Riboldsen preparing to fight a dragon (DgF 24), and Russian *byliny* habitually dwell on the details of warriors' luxurious dress. Thus, Stenka Rasin's boatmen, who are anything but overdelicate in their behavior, nevertheless wear velvet-trimmed sable caps, damask caftans, profusely interwoven coats, neatly trimmed silk shirts, and boots of morocco leather.[4] While the singers of the *Romancero* apparently wished to participate in the joys of sensuous description, they had to find a way of preserving the almost ascetic image of the Christian warrior. This they accomplished by enumerating the magnificent garments of the Moorish adversary, as in *Prim.* 72:

Reduán pide mil hombres,   el rey cinco mil le daba.
Por esa puerta de Elvira   sale muy gran cabalgada.
¡Cuánto del hidalgo moro!   ¡Cuánta de la yegua baya!
¡Cuánto de la lanza en puño!   ¡Cuánta de la adarga blanca!
¡Cuánta de marlota verde!   ¡Cuánta aljuba de escarlata!
¡Cuánta de pluma y gentileza!   ¡Cuánto capellar de grana!
¡Cuánto bayo borceguí!   ¡Cuánto lazo que le esmalta!
¡Cuánta de la espuela de oro!   ¡Cuánta estribera de plata!

Several *romances* tell about sumptuously outfitted Moors who challenge Christian knights but are defeated. It may well be that the impressive appearance of the Moor enhanced, for the audience, the valor of the Christian knight who vanquished him.

It is interesting to note that those countries that appear to delight in extended descriptions of costly clothing of heroes and heroines have also produced, as a counterbalance, ballads condemning or ridiculing vanity and ostentation—a topic not found in traditional *romances*. For example, a Breton girl who spends her time admiring her new white dress instead of going to Mass is carried away by the devil. Maidens fall prey to abduction and seduction because of their weakness for costly clothes in German, Swiss, Lithuanian, and Piedmontese ballads. The efforts of a French servant who dresses in her best, wanting to equal her lady in beauty, are thwarted by an apothecary who sells her shoe polish instead of makeup. Diuk Stepanovich, in a *bylina,* has to undergo prolonged trials because he has been bragging about his luxurious clothes. The Germanic killer of girls, known as Halewijn, Gert Olbert, etc., is, in some versions, beheaded by his intended victim as he is taking off his fine robe to keep it from being soiled by the girl's blood.[5] Proud Lady Margaret (Child 47 B) is chidden for her vanity by her dead brother, who returns from his grave:

> "When ye're in the gude church set,
>   The gowd pins in your hair,
> Ye take mair delight in your feckless dress
>   Than ye do in your mony prayer."

In contrast, the Spanish girl who walks in her finery along the meadows displays not so much sinful vanity as youthful flair and self-assurance:

> Por aquellos campos verdes   ¡qué galana iba la niña!
> Llevaba saya de grana,   jubón broslado traía;
> el zapato pica en verde,   las calzas de lana fina,
> con los sus morenos ojos   amiraba a quien la mira.
> Mirábala un caballero,   traidor, que la pretendía.
>   (Menéndez y Pelayo, 10:100)

Even though her behavior is provocative, the girl remains unscathed. She kills her assailant with his own sword and promises to mourn and bury him—an ending devoid of any trace of censure of her vanity.

Nor do the heroines in the *Romancero* lose any of their moral stature by donning their most becoming clothes to achieve political objectives. The

Cid advises his daughter (*Prim.* 55) to dress in holiday garb in order to detain the Moorish king:

> —Venid vos acá, mi hija,   mi hija doña Urraca,
> dejad las ropas continas   y vestid ropas de pascua.
> Aquel moro hi-de-perro   detenémelo en palabras,
> mientras yo ensillo a Babieca   y me ciño la mi espada.

More examples of the peculiarities of the *Romancero* will be offered in the discussion of specific moments in the life cycle, which follows. As for now, the hero or heroine has been singled out from the crowd as beautiful, financially and emotionally secure; empowered to exercise a hereditary, civil, or official status; self-confident; courageous; and determined—all this by means of basically one single symbol: clothing. The same symbol is also capable of following the protagonist from cradle to grave, through diverse relationships and crises.

An anguished princess wants her lover to smuggle her clandestinely born baby out of the palace, but first wraps the child in silk and scarlet (Bénichou, *Romancero,* p. 77). The reason may be practical: whoever the future foster parents are, they will recognize the high birth of the child. Yet the costly wraps may also be a loving or an expiatory gesture on the part of the mother. Most likely the brief line synthesizes both aspects, as also in the somewhat fanciful *Hijo vengador*:

> Van días y vienen días   y la reina pare un infante;
> toda la corte se alegra   y el rey muy apesarante;
> envolvióle en seda y grana   y a la leona se le fue a dare.
> La leona, como le vido,   conoció sangre reale,
> quitó leche a sus hijos   y al infante se la fue a dare.
> (Larrea, 2:87)

Conversely, a child ill-clothed is a child unrecognized. Prince Heathen (Child 104) subjects Lady Margaret to many injuries and indignities, but she will not weep until she has to wrap her baby son in the prince's horse-sheet. The prince then ends her trials and orders their son to be washed in milk and rolled in silk—that is, raised to his rightful position.

While lack of clothes sometimes may be a realistic evidence of neglect, as in the Piedmontese *Madre risuscitata,* where a stepmother leaves a boy out-of-doors without hat or shoes (Nigra, p. 245), more often loss of clothes signifies loss of dignity, status, or even identity. When the false steward takes from the Lord of Lorn (Child 271) his velvet gown, crimson hose, cordovan shoes, satin doublet, shirtband wrought with glistering gold, golden chain, velvet hat with a feather, and silk shirt with golden seams, and makes him wear a leather suit, the boy cannot but obey the command to change his name: he has been robbed of his identity along with his clothes.

The many ways in which a gentleman can please his lady are often symbolized by his elaborate dress. Thus, the Portuguese Dom Aleixo prepares for a midnight tryst: "Seu capacete de grana, seu chapeu á bizarria./Pegando na sua espada foi para vêr sua amiga" (Braga, *Romanceiro geral*, p. 41). In Spanish, the *romances* of the Carolingian cycle show a predilection for voluptuous dressing scenes on such occasions. After spending a sleepless night thinking of princess Claraniña, Count Claros (*Prim.* 190) jumps from his bed and demands from his valet his clothes:

> Diérale calzas de grana,   borceguís de cordobán;
> diérale jubón de seda   aforrado en zarzahán;
> diérale un manto rico   que no se puede apreciar;
> trescientas piedras preciosas   al derredor del collar.

After all this courtly refinement, however, the symbolic essence of clothing, that is, physical beauty, is revealed by the startling directness of the princess's reaction: "¡Cómo habéis hermoso cuerpo . . . !"
The metonymic nature of the descriptions of clothing is even more obvious in a modern version of *Gerineldo*:

> Por los jardines del rey,   cortando rosas y lirios,
> se pasea Gerineldo   muy calzado y muy vestido;
> lleva vestidos de seda   y zapatos de oro fino.
> La infantina para verle   a los jardines ha ido.
> —Qué lindo vas, Gerineldo,   qué galante y qué pulido;
> quién te tuviera de noche   dos horas a mi servicio.
>   (Cossío and Maza, 1:131)

Thus, while the knight's eye-catching dress may be a sign of serving and obeying his lady—sometimes even prescribed by her, as in *Will Stewart and John* (Child 107) or *Toros y cañas* (Cossío and Maza, 2:32-33)—it can be often deciphered as a legitimate way of circumventing the taboo of direct mention of physical attraction.

An unmistakably erotic function, however, is assigned to incomplete dress. In *Melisenda* (*Prim.* 198), the lovesick princess jumps out of bed on a sleepless night and, taking time only to throw on her shirt, sets out to invade the bedchamber of Count Ayruelo:

> Todas las gentes dormían   en las que Dios tiene parte,
> mas no duerme la Melisenda,   la hija del emperante;
> que amores del conde Ayruelo   no la dejan reposar.
> Salto diera de la cama   como la parió su madre,
> vistiérase una alcándora   no hallando su brial.

An even better known variant of this motif creates a heavily sensual climate in the truncated *Mora Moraima* (*Prim.* 132), where a Moorish girl in dishabille rushes to open the door for the shrewd Christian who pretends to be her uncle:

> Si no me abres tú, mi vida,   aquí me verás matar.
> Cuando esto oí, cuitada,   comencéme a levantar,
> vistiérame una almejía   no hallando mi brial,
> fuérame para la puerta   y abríla de par en par.

A similarly suggestive atmosphere pervades a Serbian ballad, where a love charm wrought by the widower Ali compels proud Emina, clad only in a thin shirt, to come at midnight to his gate (Eisner, p. 389).

That the motif of incomplete dress has mainly an erotic meaning is borne out not only by the unequivocal contexts but also by the fact that a different commonplace is used where only haste or anxiety needs to be expressed. In Spanish, the respective formula is, "si de prisa se vestía,   más de prisa se calzaba," or "de prisa pide el vestido,   de prisa pide el calzado"; in Portuguese, "com uma mão se vestia,   com a outra se calçava"; all of which correspond to a British commonplace with numerous variants, such as "She's taen her mantle her about,/her coffer by the hand."[6]

Even though the custom appears to have been similar in many European countries, the *Romancero* offers only indirect evidence of the traditional engagement gifts: a shirt sewn and embroidered by the girl for the man;

shoes—often also a dress and jewelry—from the man to the girl. The refusal by a girl to make a shirt, or by a man to accept it, is tantamount to a refusal of marriage. A correspondingly binding significance is attached to shoes: if the girl once accepts them and no wedding follows, she considers herself deceived.[7]

Balladists have frequently made use of these customs in order to enlarge upon the evolution and crises of a love relationship. The Scottish *False Lover Won Back* (Child 218 B) juxtaposes by means of contradictory pairs of verses the gradual change of heart and the verbal implacability of the young man who is determined to leave his sweetheart:

> The firsten town that they came to,
>   He bought her hose and sheen,
> And bade her rue and return again,
>   And gang nae farther wi him.
> . . . .
> The nexten town that they came to,
>   He bought her a brand new gown,
> And bade her rue and return again,
>   And gang nae farther wi him.
>
> The nexten town that they came to,
>   He bought her a wedding ring,
> And bade her dry her rosy cheeks,
>   And he would tak her wi him.

A similar sequence in a French ballad elaborates the happiness of the young couple after overcoming the obstacles created by the girl's father:

> La première ville,
> Son amant l'habille
> Tout en satin blanc.
> La seconde ville,
> Son amant l'habille
> En or et argent.
> . . . .
> La troisième ville,
> Son amant l'habille
> En épousement.
> El étoit si belle,
> Quel passoit pour reine
> Dans le régiment.
>   (Doncieux, pp. 426-27)

A few scattered *romances* suggest a comparable factual background in the Hispanic world. The greedy girl in the modern *Pedigüeña* scorns a student's proposal: "Niña, si usted me quisiera   por el término de un año/la calzara y la vistiera   y la regalara un paño" (Cossío and Maza, 2:107). The significance of a shirt, unequivocally demonstrated in European ballads, can be detected in the Sephardic *¿Por qué no cantáis, la bella?*:

> Una hija tiene el rey,   que la tiene arreglada;
> su padre por más favor   un castillo la fraguara . . .
> Labrando está un camisón   para el hijo de la reina;
> labrándolo está con oro,   pespunteándolo con seda,
> y entre pespunte y pespunte   un aljófar y una perla.
> (Menéndez Pidal, "Romancero
> judío-español," no. 57)

In the Catalan *Peregrina,* a shirt retrieves a wayward lover: when Joan finds out that María, his former sweetheart, sewed and embroidered the splendid shirt that the queen pretends to have made for him, he leaves the queen and returns to María (Milá, pp. 181-82). It is unlikely, however, that the value of the garment or the superior sewing skill was the decisive factor; the appreciation of a tangible object, easily imaginable in its visual aspect, symbolizes the reactivation of a temporarily suppressed emotion. Similarly, the Piedmontese Margherita's hyperbolic description of her fiancé's gift—a dress of thirty-three colors, made by three tailors—is probably not meant to express a calculating preference for a wealthy husband, but is a way of telling the new pretender that there is a lovebond he cannot hope to break (Nigra, p. 403).

Scandinavian balladists obviously have the custom of engagement gifts in mind as they display the fantastic lure of the fairy world: elf-maids trying to entice knights with silk shirts, boots of buckskin, golden spurs, helmets, and swords (DgF 47, 48). In one of the Scandinavian *viser* a horse and a magnificent ship are added to the promise, and the Catalan version of *Rosaflorida* enlarges the offer from clothes embroidered with gold and silver to two castles, each manned by a hundred soldiers, if only the beloved knight would come (Milá, p. 248).

Already in the last examples, the lavish offers go beyond a token engagement gift and become instruments of seduction—a function that stands out clearly in the modern *Canción de una gentil dama y un rústico pastor*:

—Tú que estás acostumbrado   a ponerte esos sajones;
si te casaras conmigo   te pusieras pantalones.
· ·
—Tú, que estás acostumbrado   a ponerte chamarreta;
si te casaras conmigo,   te pondrías tu chaqueta.[8]

When a girl is to be seduced, however, the lure in the *Romancero* seldom
is anything more specific than the stereotyped (but far from meaningless)
gold and silver clothing:

—Delgadina, Delgadida,   la mi hija más delgada,
si tú lo quisieras ser   la mi hija enamorada,
yo te vestiría de oro   te calzaría de plata.
(Cossío and Maza, 1:305)

Another incest ballad, *Silvana,* begins in a similar manner: "¡Qué bien te
cae, Silvana, la ropa de todos los días;/mejor que la reina, tu
madre,   de oro y plata la traerías!" (Cossío and Maza, 1:291).

In contrast, British (*Redesdale and Wise William,* Child 246; *James
Harris,* Child 243) and, particularly, Scandinavian ballads dwell with rel-
ish on the successive offers:

"O Kirstin, fair Kirstin, come trip it with me;
I've a gown all of silk, and I'll give it to thee."

"For gown all of silk, sir—as good I can buy,
But dance not this year with the King's son will I."[9]

Kirstin refuses also shoes latched with silver, a golden buckle, half a gold
ring, and knives hilted with silver, but drops her resistance at the promise
of honor and troth. In the Danish version of the legend of Saint Catherine,
the prince's offers begin with seven silk-embroidered dresses and culminate in a fort, a castle, and a crown of gold—all of which are refused, as
the girl chooses a martyr's death (DgF 101).

Quite logically, the cost and number of the gifts depend largely upon the
kind of proposal that they accompany—the extravagance of seducers of
both sexes outshines the symbolic gifts exchanged by those intending to
marry. A notable difference exists also between countries and languages,
the customs of the Spanish *Romancero,* as usual, appearing to be the least
opulent.

The contrast between the reticence of Hispanic *romances* and the prolixity of other ballads in elaborating the clothing motif in the wooing of girls is paralleled in the description of wedding clothes. Other than a *romance* about the Cid's wedding, published in 1600 (thus not in the *Romancero viejo*), which inserts in the praise of Rodrigo's and Jimena's traditional dress a censure of contemporary aberrations, a few variants of a burlesque song about the cat's nuptials contain perhaps the only noteworthy Spanish elaboration of wedding attire: "Estaba el señor gato   en silla de oro sentado,/calzando medias de seda,   zapatos blancos bordados." A Chilean variant lacks details about Mr. Cat, but describes his bride-to-be: "Llegó la señora Gata   con vestido muy planchado,/con mediecitas de seda   y zapatos rebajados."[10]

In many other countries, ballads dwell with obvious pleasure on the dressing of the bride. Thus, the Danish *Jon rømmer af Land*:

> She decked herself in a silken sark,
> That was of nine maidens the handiwork.

> She decked herself in a mantle of blue,
> At every seam the red gold shone through.

> Ring after ring did Kirsteen don,
> On every finger they shimmered and shone.

> With ribbons of silk and golden crown
> She decked her tresses that hung adown.[11]

Even an unwilling bride such as Fair Janet (Child 64), quoted earlier, who has to marry an old French lord, chooses a scarlet dress, which lets her outshine all others, dressed in green or brown. Just as loath is the Finnish Aino to marry old Väinämöinen, but the wedding clothes are urged upon her by her mother—an opportunity of which the singer makes the most: six gold belts; seven blue dresses, woven by Moon Spirit, finished off by Sun Spirit; a sheer linen shirt; a fine wool dress; a silk belt; fine silk stockings; beautiful shoes with ornamented uppers; ribbons for the hair; gold rings and bracelets. The wedding clothes are enumerated again when Aino takes them off to swim to a rock, from which she slips into the water and drowns: "She threw her shirt on a willow, her dress on an aspen, her stockings on the sandy shore."[12]

Without losing any of the sensuous enjoyment that is evident in the foregoing passages, the description of the clothing of the bride's rival takes on additional functions in the dramatic plot of several ballads. The theme of the deserted girl who goes to the wedding and in the last hour of her life outshines the bride is found in many countries, but whatever the national differences, the dressing of the abandoned sweetheart is an obbligato episode. Much has been made of the paradox of the girl's poverty—in many versions the reason for her being abandoned—and her gorgeous dress.[13] If, however, some passages in Child 73 E, as an example, are considered in their respective contexts, the seeming contradiction disappears. While the young man is undecided which girl to marry, he is told by his mother:

> "The nut-brown maid has sheep and cows,
>   And Fair Annie has nane;
> And Willie, for my benison,
>   The nut-brown maid bring hame."

The subsequent stanzas deal mainly with Annie's preparations for attending her faithless truelove's wedding. He sends word to her not to wear black or brown, "But the scarlet sae red, and the kerches sae white,/And your bonny locks hanging down." She has maidens lay gold in her hair, tailors make her a weed, and smiths shoe her a steed. Significantly, though, the description of her arrival in church focuses not on the details of her dress but on the effect of her appearance:

> And whan she came to Mary-kirk,
>   And sat down in the deas,
> The light that came frae Fair Annie
>   Enlightened a' the place.

The nut-brown bride, in dismay, turns to her father:

> "If that be Willie's first true-love,
>   He might hae latten me be;
> She has as much gold on ae finger
>   As I'll wear till I die."

It is easy to see why the ballad has been accused of being paradoxical, since it might seem that Annie is wealthier than the nut-brown bride. However, we are led back to the right track by the nut-brown bride's pointed question, which is not about Annie's dress or jewelry, but her fair face:

> "O whare got ye that water, Annie,
>   That washes you sae white?"

The dazzling attire was, thus, nothing but a coded exaltation of Annie's beauty. (The pattern is the same as in the other ballads analyzed earlier, such as *La cautiva,* where the captive princess arrived dressed in gold and silver, but was sent to do laundry in a cold spring, so that she would lose her coloring.) Noteworthy also is the two-stage metonymy in several texts of Child 73: from the array of the horse to that of the rider, and finally to the latter's natural beauty. In some variants, the girl's clothes show that she is the true match for Thomas: they are dressed either in the same (Child 73 D-e) or in complementary colors: "He dressed himself up in a suit of green,/And his merrymen all in white," and "She dressed herself in a suit of white,/And her merrymen all in green" (Child 73 D-g). Thus the clothing of Fair Annet, far from incongruous, is an expression of the basic facts on which the story is constructed.

It would be equally beside the point to censure the lack of realism in the French counterpart, *Tristes noces,* which shows the girl changing her dress after each round of the dance. The purpose of the extended passages about the girl's gowns is to convince the audience of her beauty and—beautiful being equal to good—of her right to be married to the man. At the same time, the dressing scene shows the determination of the girl to prove to the faithless man his mistake, and to prove it before the whole congregation— a psychological process, which, in keeping with the usage in ballads, is translated into visual and tactile terms. The clothing of the abandoned sweetheart has functions integral to the plot of this group of ballads; the verses about the poor girl's finery need not be excused as merely reflecting the "childlike pleasure of the populace in color and splendor"—the explanation given by Pohl (p. 81).

A search for a correspondingly elaborate description in the *Romancero viejo* would doubtless lead to *La bella en misa,* even though in most texts more verses deal with the lady's physical features or cosmetics than with her clothing (in *Prim.* 143, the latter is limited to "saya lleva sobre saya,   mantillo de un tornasol"). Entwistle's hypothesis about the origins of this *romance* in the Neo-Hellenic *Bridesmaid into Bride* has been substantiated by Armistead and Silverman.[14] Keeping in mind, however, that those scholars were seeking to establish a genealogical line for *La bella en misa,* while the present analysis deals with the function of clothing in each ballad as such, it would be precipitate to conclude that the attire of the lady in the *romance* has the same meaning as the clothing in the European ballads of bridal rivalry, including the Greek song. The Spanish texts

preserve only some enigmatic fragments of a narrative and have been attached, in the modern tradition, to other *romances* with plots quite different from that either of *Bridesmaid into Bride* (where the stunningly
dressed concubine triumphs over the lady who has temporarily displaced
her) or of the *Lord Thomas-Tristes noces* group (where the abandoned
sweetheart usually dies, after disrupting the wedding).[15] *La bella en misa*
has even inspired a parody: "En cada zapato lleva   vara y media de
tacón;/en cada carrillo lleva   onza y media de color" (Schindler, texts, p.
65).

From the foregoing, one might almost conclude that the Hispanic tradition has divorced the reference to clothing from the story of the abandoned sweetheart (*El veneno de Moriana* is close to the latter in its plot,
but lacks a description of Moriana's attire), were it not for the little-known
Sofía mía, preserved in New Mexico, which has the earmarks of a *romance
viejo* and does include a line that shows affinity to the clothing scene:

—¿Qué dices, Anita Rica,   qué dices, Sofía mía?
—Que el Duque se anda casando   con otra y a mí me olvida.
Sofía se fue a su casa   muy triste, muy pensativa,
con sus bracitos cruzados   sus anillos le lucían.
Sofía se fue al jardín   muy triste, muy pensativa;
ya vido venir al Duque   con toda su compañía.[16]

The duke invites Sofía to his wedding, whereupon she dies and is mourned
by him until his death fifteen years later. In a typically Hispanic form—
more succinct and stylized than, for example, the British or the Scandinavian—*Sofía mía* tells essentially the same story as *Tristes noces*. The suicide is replaced by the languishing of the duke, a difference that may be
observed also between other Spanish and non-Spanish ballads (contrast
Venganza de honor with *Il Corsaro* or *L'embarquement de la fille*).[17] Likewise the contrast between the brief "con sus bracitos cruzados   sus anillos
le lucían" and the detailed descriptions in other languages falls within the
regular differences that may be observed in numerous ballads; as pointed
out earlier, lines like "de oro calzada,   de plata ceñida" are the Spanish
counterpart of extended passages in ballads of other countries. In songs
that deal with a successful claim of the first wife or betrothed, such as the
British *Young Beichan* (Child 53), the description of the luxurious outfit
of the winner is repeated several times, while the silk shift revealed by the
Spanish condesita under her pilgrim's cloak serves its purpose with one

brief mention. Competition in dress appears to be sufficient justification for a whole French song, *Je suis allée aux noces,* where the married wedding guest who outshines the bride seems to lack any sentimental motives (Canteloube, 4:256).

At the same time, Sofia's rings have a counterpart in the gold that the Scandinavian groom has at one time given to Kirsten and forbids her to wear to his wedding. Furthermore, in their discussion of the relationship of *La bella en misa* and the Greek song about competing brides, Armistead and Silverman quote pertinent lines from the Extremeño version of the former:

> Y en sus manos blancas lleva   anillos de gran való[r],
> que se los trajo su amante,   que se los trajo su amó[r],
> que se los trajo su amante   de la feria de León.[18]

Also a Sephardic text of this *romance* mentions rings: "En sus manos catorce anillos   que la misa esclandeció" (Larrea, 2:102). Since *Sofía mía,* as it exists, lacks a wedding scene, the rings have no immediately recognizable function, but may well have been the symbol of Sofía's superior beauty—and her superior right to the duke—in some earlier versions that elaborated the competition. Perhaps they were also a binding gift from the duke. The similarity between the references to rings in the other songs and in *Sofía mía* points to a similar significance. With the syncopation of the story and the omission of the wedding (assuming that there was one in a longer version), the mention of rings—having lost its narrative context—may have moved toward the beginning of the *romance*, as quoted here.

In summary, the foregoing examples point to a multiple connection among *La bella en misa, Sofía mía,* and the large European group of *Lord Thomas-Tristes noces,* all of which employ clothing in the form typical of each linguistic group.

The wife's deceptively simple description of the absent husband (in the likewise deceptively entitled *Señas del marido*) is, in essence, not so much an identification of the man as a declaration of love and fidelity by the wife:

> Mi marido es blanco y rubio   y alto como una ciprés;
> lleva la media de seda   y çapatito de babel.
> (Bénichou, *Romancero,* p. 227)

Although this *romance* mentions also several physical features, the lines about clothing are an important part of the subjective aspect of the wife's opinion: to her, he is the most handsome of all.

For a husband's love, one of the frequent symbols in the code of ballads is the providing of luxurious dress for his wife. In Scandinavian *viser*, clothes of scarlet and sable for a wife mean a happy marriage (DgF 23, 75, 78, 408). In the Spanish *Condesita,* quoted earlier, the count's order to dress his wife in gold and silk is fundamentally a promise to make up for past neglect. Well-intended promises may occasionally, however, run into obstacles, as in *La dama pastora.* Mariana, abducted by don Güeso, wants to turn back for her clothes, but he assures her that his mother will lend her what she needs. When he leaves her in his mother's care, she becomes a mistreated daughter-in-law who has to dress in rags. Fairly enough, she is vindicated when she refuses to put on a silk dress for a guest—who later turns out to be her husband—and thus reveals how ill she has been faring in his absence. In the French version of this ballad, *La Porcheronne,* the mother-in-law has allowed her own daughters to wear the fine dresses and jewelry of the young wife, while the latter has been wearing coarse clothes.[19]

It is quite revealing that ballad singers have found it necessary to compound the crime of the Halewijn-Ulinger ilk by having the homicidal "lover" demand the victim's clothes for another woman. In some versions of the German *Mädchenmörder* that end with the villain's hanging, the girl's brother gets even with him by demanding his clothes for a page or a kitchen-boy.[20] The assassin's attitude toward the girl's clothes seems to prove beyond doubt that he was not husband material.

The same basic idea—that clothes mean happy life—is expressed in another way when the Portuguese countess, whose husband has been ordered to kill her, takes leave of her mirror that has served her for dressing: "Adeos espelho real   onde me via e vestia;/Que ámanhã por estas horas   ja estarei na terra fria" (Braga, *Romanceiro geral,* p. 70). In a different context, the Lass of Roch Royal (Child 76 D) expresses by means of clothing symbolism her longing for a happy marriage:

> "O wha will shoe my fu fair foot?
> An wha will glove my han?
> An wha will lace my middle gimp
> Wi the new made London ban?"

On the other hand, good treatment is not always appreciated. When Escrivana flees from the Moorish castle, the Moor laments having dressed her for seven years in silk and ivory.[21] In a Serbian ballad, Ajkuna's brother gives her to the old Mustapha, who will clothe her in silk and satin, but Ajkuna elopes from the wedding procession with young Suko (Bowring, p. 30). The Breton Tina feels an intense dislike for the old Baron of Jauioz; when he offers her a mantle of state, she would rather have a linen skirt made by her mother (La Villemarqué, p. 208). The Scottish Jeanie, who loves Auchanachie but must marry Salton (Child 239), pleads with her father:

> "Wi Auchanachie Gordon I would beg my bread
> Before that wi Salton I'd wear gowd on my head,
> Wear gowd on my head, or gowns fring'd to the knee;
> And I'll die if I getna my love Auchanachie."

As was the case with engagement gifts, to scorn the clothes is to scorn the man and his love. On the one hand, the prospective costly dress assures the audience of the husband's sincere affection; on the other, the rejection of the clothes denotes an emotional block on the part of the woman, without casting a shadow on the man's character. He may be worthy of love, but she cannot love him.

Gifts of clothing are likewise the balladists' favorite choice among all the possible proofs of adultery. In the Sephardic *Mujer engañada,* the wife vents her wrath by locking out her husband, after overhearing him promise his paramour expensive clothes:

> "Tú eres mi bien,   tú eres mi vida,
> que a la otra mujere   yo no la quería;
> y a ti te compraré   paños y mantillas,
> y a la otra mujer   palos y mala vida."
> (Larrea, 1:258)

Even the clothes given to a woman before the marriage to another appear to be sufficient evidence of a husband's disloyalty. The Danish Tove is a combination of the wronged sweetheart who outshines the bride, and the royal favorite who, by flaunting the tangible proof of her advantage, arouses the ire of the legitimate wife. Tove, King Valdemar's faithful consort of many years, goes to pay a call on the queen Valdemar has newly brought home. After a pointed remark about Tove's gorgeous dress with silken train, the queen asks what the king gave Tove as a morning gift and receives a vexing answer:

> "He clad me in silk and scarlet gay,
> Thou and all thy maidens ne'er go in such array."
> (DgF 121, trans. Smith-Dampier, p. 136)

On Christmas Day, when the queen sees Tove go to church in silk and samite, she invites her rival to a bath and kills her by overheating the bathhouse—an act that costs her the king's favor.

Women who misread the signs and see evil where there is none are usually stepmothers or mothers-in-law. The dress of Lady Isabel (Child 261) spurs her stepmother to accuse her of incest with her father:

> "It may be very well seen, Isabel,
> It may be very well seen;
> He buys to you the damask gowns,
> To me the dowie green."

The circumstances are similar in the Sephardic *Mala suegra castigada*:

> Mujer de don Pedro   y a la Misa iría
> vestida de verde   y en la grana fina.
> Su suegro, el buen rey,   mucho la quería;
> su suegra es muy mala,   zelos la entraría.
> (Larrea, 1:234)

The jealous mother-in-law tells her son to kill his wife, but has to pay with her own life. As in the previous example, it is clear that the clothes are not the cause of suspicion and hostility but rather the sanctioned code for expressing such feelings in a popular ballad. The visible evidence is the same in ballads that deal with real intent of incest (*Delgadina, Silvana*) or adultery (*Mujer engañada*); whether or not the gift or offer of fine clothes is indeed a sign of illicit relationships depends in each case on the characters and the plot. The false accusations made by Lady Isabel's stepmother or don Pedro's mother stem from their consistent attitude toward a stepdaughter or daughter-in-law and find in clothing not their cause, but their poetic expression.

A similar chain of reasoning obviously must be applied to clothing as a manifestation of a happy marriage. Although a generous clothing allowance may well be an important part of a loving attitude proper to a good husband, it would be far too simplistic to limit such an attitude to this particular aspect. The language of balladry usually shuns abstractions, particularly such complex concepts as the quality of a marriage, gradual psychological processes, or conjectures; clothing offers itself as a natural substitute for such discourses. That ballad characters do not give analytical speeches in the verbatim text does not mean that they possess only a rudimentary emotional structure. Since both the balladist and the audience have a key to the code, the latter will fill in the subtle psychological development that the words of the song have omitted. The listeners may find a clue even in such a formal difference as that between direct and indirect speech. In the ballads where a character makes a direct offer to another, the clothing is indeed likely to show an existent feeling or desire, as in the *Delgadina, Silvana, Mujer engañada,* or in the German *Vorwirt,* in which the dead husband sends word to his remarried wife that his clothes have rotted in the grave, and she compassionately exclaims: "Ich möcht ihm eins abschneiden/von Sammet und von Seiden!" (*Deutsche Volkslieder,* 5:9). In contrast, an observation made by a third party, particularly an interested one, tends to express the feelings of the observer rather than those of the wearer or the donor of the clothes.

The same distinction can be made when a man and a woman together are said to be wearing fine clothes. In *Jamie Douglas* (Child 204), the wife describes her happy marriage in terms of the clothing that each was wearing:

> I was a lady of high renown
> As lived in the north countrie;
> I was a lady of high renown
> Whan Earl Douglas loved me.
>
> Whan we cam through Glasgow toun,
> We war a comely sight to see;
> My gude lord in velvet green,
> And I mysel in cramasie.
>
> Whan we cam to Douglas toun,
> We war a fine sight to behold;
> My gude lord in cramasie,
> And I myself in shining gold.

If the couple are not married to each other, however, their wearing of fine dress would imply adultery, and slanderous reports to that effect may cause calamity. Envious courtiers in *Nacimiento de Montesinos* succeed in having the count exiled by falsely informing the king of a meeting between the count and the queen, each in fine array: "Que le vieran con la reina   en sus palacios reales;/el conde, jubón de seda;   la reina, ricos briales" (Larrea, 1:105).

The function of festive clothing as a sign of a love relationship extends also to ballads where only the dress of a woman is mentioned, as in *La esposa de don García*. In this *romance*, the events described as accompanied by contrasting clothes are mutually exclusive; only one or the other can be true. Don García's mother says his wife went gladly with the Moors; the wife's mother (in one variant her, or don García's, aunt) says she was abducted against her will. As proof of her attitude, they offer conflicting testimony about her playing or not playing the viol, about the way she talked to the Moors, and about the kind of dress she wore:

His mother	The aunt:
—Por aquí pasó esta noche	—Por aquí pasó esta noche
dos horas antes del día,	tres horas antes del día,
vestida de colorado	toda vestida de negro
que una reina parecía,	que una viuda parecía,
vihuela de oro en sus manos,	vihuela de oro en las manos,
y muy bien que la tangía.	de pesar no la tangía;
Cada vuelta que le daba,	cada vuelta que le daba,
cuernos, cuernos, don García.	¡valme, valme, don García![22]

If she had gone willingly with the Moors (as it turns out, she did not), perhaps she could have indeed dressed in her holiday best, but a woman abducted against her will would hardly have an opportunity to procure mourning clothes to show her protest. Her black dress is clearly a poetic device—a concrete, visual image that takes the place of a description of the wife's emotional state.

Even the erotic connotation of a wife's opening the door in a state of undress lacks in the *Romancero* the most obvious function of being caught *in flagrante delicto* (as it has in some Russian *byliny*), but serves primarily as a poetic code for the woman's emotions, as in the highly sensuous Portuguese *Dom Pedro Françoilo*:

> Pois se erguera d'onde estava   descalsa lhe fôra abrir,
> Lhe pegara pela mão   o levára ao seu jardim;
> Lhe lavára pés e mãos   com bella agua de alecrim;
> Uma gota que ficara   lavára tambem a si,

Vestira-lhe uma camisa   como quem vestira a si,
Fizera cama de rosas,   o deitara a par de si.
                                    (Braga, *Açoriano,* p. 205)

In fact, the Catalan counterpart of this *romance* spells out the difference: as the adulterous wife hears a knock on the door, she declares herself ready to open right away for her lover, but would take time to put on clothes and shoes if it is her husband (Milá, p. 245).

Black clothing worn at the death of someone dear, especially widow's weeds, may seem in ballads nothing more than a realistic portrayal of an actual custom, but usually reverts to its profound origin: the feeling of sincere sorrow. Thus, the husband who visits his wife incognito and gives her the false news of his own death is convinced of her constancy—and not just of her conventionality—when she puts on mourning: "A otro día de mañana,   madrugó a misa primera;/iba vestida de luto   de los pies a la cabeza." Already somewhat stylized is the appearance of the wife at the husband's deathbed in *Muerte del príncipe don Juan:* "Ellos en estas palabras,   su esposa por la puerta entrara,/una soga en la garganta   y un velo negro en la cara." Even further removed is the cause from the effect when Bernaldo del Carpio chooses black clothes and a black horse before rushing to stop the dishonorable execution of his father: "Íbase por un camino   el valiente Don Bernaldo;/todo vestido de luto,   negro también el caballo." Verjicos is neither dead nor dying, only imprisoned by the king, but Isabel dresses herself and her ladies-in-waiting in mourning: "Un día indo el rey a caza   se encontró con una mujer;/todo iba vestida de luto,   ella, y sus damas también." Still less realism can be found in the black robe of a hurried messenger—a Moor at that—as he brings the king of Granada the grim news of the advance of the Christian troops: "Ese que primero llega   es ese Cegrí nombrado,/con una marlota negra,   señal de luto mostrando."[23] Of the five examples above, only the first can be classified as a reproduction of a custom that expresses also the true psychological state of the supposed widow. In the other four, the black of mourning is used with poetic license; the black on the visual scene conveys the emotion of sorrow or foreshadows a grave state of affairs that may come to cause sorrow.

If we return to the conventional widow's weeds, we see that the ballad singer often is not content to show just the black clothes, but prefers a strong contrast, usually white and black. A version of the *romance* of the return of the husband recites the vow of the supposed widow: "Voy quitar mi toca blanca; voy poner mi toca negra,/lutar puertas y ventanas, y también las escaleras" (Menéndez y Pelayo, 10:138). The seeking of contrast is even more obvious when Teresa, hearing that her sweetheart Francisco has been gored by a bull, dresses in white to visit him, but, halfway there, hears the tolling of bells and demands mourning clothes:

> —Déme usté el vestido blanco, voy a verle la cornada.
> A la mitad del camino oyó tocar las campanas.
> —Déme usté el vestido, madre, de luto que no de gala.
> (Cossío and Maza, 2:72)

A similar change from gay colors to mourning, this time in the clothes of a man, is shown in the French *Mort de la mie*:

> Ma mère, apportez-mois mes habits de soie rose,
> Et mon chapeau qu'il soit d'argent bordé:
> Je veux ma mie aller trouver.
> . . . .
> Ma mère, apportez-moi mon habit de soie noire,
> Et mon chapeau qu'il soit de crêpe bordé:
> Le deuil d'amour je veux porter.
> (Tiersot, pp. 116-17)

The juggling of colors can sometimes express concepts more intricate than a simple turn of events. In the numerous versions, from many countries, of the ballad about the young wife from whom the news of her husband's death is withheld while she is in childbed, her choice of clothes for Mass is the vehicle for pathos, suspense, and dramatic irony. The mother-in-law (as well as the audience) knows of the death and tries to persuade the widow to dress in black. A pathetic effect is achieved by the unknowing widow's insistence on wearing gay colors:

> —Diga, diga la mi suegra, ¿qué vestido llevaría?
> —Como eres alta y delgada lo negro bien te estaría.
> —Yo no quiero llevar luto que voy de linda parida.
> (Menéndez y Pelayo, 10:111)

In some variants where the widow goes to Mass in colors, her clothes give rise to comment: "Encontraron un pastor que de su hato volvía:/—¡Qué viudita tan hermosa;　　viuda y de grana vestida!''[24] The widow, dressed in red, learns of the death of her husband through a remark made about her clothing:

> Pasó por ahí un caballero　que a doña Ana malquería.
> Vistan de luto a doña Ana　que don Bueso muerto había.
> Doña Ana de que esto oyó,　desmayada se caía.
> 　　　　　　　(Cossío and Maza, 1:208-9)

The French equivalent of this ballad, *Le Roi Renaud,* focuses gradually on the ominous color, but then postpones the climax by giving an irrelevant reason for wearing black:

> "Dites-moi, ma mére m'ami',
> Quel habit prendrai-je aujourd'hui?"
> "Prenez le vert, prenez le gris,
> Prenez le noir, pour mieus choisir."
>
> "Dites-moi, ma mére, m'ami',
> Ce que ce noir-là signifi'?"
> "Femme qui relève d'enfant,
> Le noir lui est bien plus séant."
> 　　　　　　　(Doncieux, p. 93)

In the Breton *Aotrou Nann,* the mother-in-law tells the wife it is now the fashion to wear black to church. In the Piedmontese *Morte occulta,* she says: "You in black, I in grey; we'll go according to the custom of the land."[25] The advice to wear black and the comments on the widow's gay clothing are designed to heighten the suspense: When will she realize the truth? At the same time, the contrast between the colors the widow wears, or wants to wear, and the black that is urged upon her illustrates the contrast between the unwarranted emotions and those she should have in the light of the events as yet unknown to her.

A similar effect is achieved in *Sweet William's Ghost* (Child 77 C). The counterweight of the holiday clothes that Margaret joyously anticipates is the winding-sheet of the revenant who comes to claim back his troth-plight:

> "Have ye brought me any scarlets so red?
> 　Or any silks so fine?
> Or have ye brought me any precious things,
> 　That merchants have for sale?"

> "I have not brought you any scarlets sae red,
>   No, no, nor the silks so fine;
> But I have brought you my winding sheet,
>   Oer many's the rock and hill."

In Child 229 A, the contrast of scarlet and black appears sufficient to portray the climax of the gradual change of heart and the subsequent stunning blow, as Earl Crawford, ready to relent and to take back his wife, whom he has banished in anger, receives the news of her death from her father:

> And dowie rade to the yates o Crawford,
>   And when to Crawford's yates he came,
> They were a' dressd in the robes o scarlet,
>   Just gaun to tak Lady Lillie hame.
> "Ye may cast aff your robes o scarlet—
>   I wyte they set you wondrous weel—
> And now put on the black sae dowie,
>   And come and bury your Lady Lill."

The two parts of the contrast are more loosely joined in *The Earl of Aboyne* (Child 235 A). Lady Aboyne's splendid costume denotes her happy expectation of her husband; the black-clad funeral procession—after nine intervening stanzas—illustrates the earl's remorse upon hearing that his wife has died of a broken heart because of his infidelity.

The description of emotional shock solely by visual means, and the limitation of the latter to clothing, represents a rigorous coding accomplished by the creators of the ballads, although there is little doubt that the audience will immediately retranslate the image into the original, emotional, terms. Still, the foregoing contrasts, while doubtless chosen for poetic purposes, remain at least to some extent in the realm of probability. When we turn to the Sicilian *Scibilia nobili,* the use of colors has only a tenuous connection with reality. Scibilia's father, mother, brother, and sister refused to ransom her from the Moors, so she wears at their deaths red, yellow, green, and white, respectively. Only for her husband, who was willing to part with all his gold to pay for her release, would she wear black (Jewett, p. 30). In this ballad, the gay clothes at death are—in the manner of a photographic negative—the reversal of a hypothetical image of hostility in life, the latter being the primary idea. In the same category is the humorous *romance* about the cat's death and the joy of the mice:

Y los ratones, de gusto,   se visten de colorado,
diciendo: "¡Gracias a Dios   que murió este condenado,
que nos hacía correr   con el rabito parado!"
(Vicuña, p. 133)

The game of colors allows innumerable variations. Hyperbole and realism are joined in *El desdichado,* where clothing illustrates the simultaneous contrasting emotions of two persons. The rejected suitor visualizes
the wedding day of the girl and predicts in conclusion that her wedding
will be his funeral:

El día de las tus bodas   te vestirán de encarnado
y a mí sólo me pondrán   un hábito franciscano.
Te pondrán ricos zapatos   con las hebillas de plata
y a mí sólo me pondrán   unas simples alpargatas.
(Cossío and Maza, 2:91)

In the last example, the red dress of the bride-to-be and the monk's
habit of the scorned man are clearly symbols of joy and despair, but also
connote, respectively, the proximity and the renunciation of the consum-
mation of a marriage. Not only in the most obvious cases, as those of dishabille, but in a great many others, where the wearing or offering of
clothes may seem a purely materialistic gesture, the underlying reason for
the references to clothing is the puritanical tendency observable in much of
occidental balladry. Such puritanism is often merely lexical, not factual;
nevertheless, it imposes on the ballad singer certain restrictions, which he
has to circumvent by finding acceptable substitutes for the direct mention
of taboos. Even though a considerable number of ballads deal with erotic
subjects, we seldom find patently erotic descriptions or expressions. Next
to combing (see chap. 5), clothing is the favorite symbol of sexuality—and
a symbol that can be used with impunity.

In several examples at the beginning of this discussion, the key to the
code was offered in the very verses of a ballad: physical, nubile beauty was
mentioned interchangeably with dazzling dress. The same equation is implicit in cases where the best-dressed girl is either chosen for a bride or pursued by a lecher. One can hardly believe that the Cid's daughter was able
to distract the Moorish king from his belligerent mission simply by dis-
playing her holiday costume, or that Gerineldos's silken suit and golden
footgear compelled the princess to invite him to her bedroom.

Nor must the fine clothing offered to a desirable mate be interpreted as a blatant bid to buy either legitimate or illegitimate favors in exchange for a quantity of textiles. The promise to please with gifts of clothing is an all-encompassing promise to please. For example, one cannot imagine that an elf-maid would be reticent in describing her charms to a young knight; it is the ballad singer who has to be reticent in formulating the discourse and, therefore, makes the elf-maid verbally appeal to the knight's greed instead of his lust.

As we noticed earlier, the wife who describes her absent husband's silk hose and fine shoes says in reality that she is in love with him; well-dressed couples represent mutual love. The wives who fly into a rage—even commit murder—at the sight of the sumptuous attire of their husbands' concubines surely do not envy just the material advantages of their rivals, but mainly the love-bond that the clothes symbolize. Were we to attach to the lines about clothing only their literal meaning, the strong reactions of the characters would often seem unwarranted or ridiculous. Since, however, the deeper significance of such verses is a part of common knowledge, or, more accurately, of common subconscious awareness, a danger of absurdity does not arise, and in most cases the balladists have not found it necessary to follow the mention of clothing with any more explicit passages.

The extraordinary suitability of clothing as a disguise for a taboo would alone be sufficient to overrule a certain incompatibility with the customary modes of expression in ballads, which prefer action to description. It should be interjected here, however, that action is not necessarily lacking, since clothing can be joined to verbs of action. Often each piece is described while a person is dressing himself or is being dressed by another. In some cases, past motion is reflected in the finished action: a person is dressed, that is, he has dressed or has been dressed. In Spanish the element of motion is sometimes restored by the proximity of a verb ("vestida en blanco venía"; "la llevan cautiva de oro calzada"). Then again, past action may be recalled by telling who made the garment ("la mora que la labrara   por su amiga la tenía"; "las cien damas lo tejieron   a la sombra del lunar").

While, even so, the kinetic element remains modest, another stylistic convention of balladry—visuality—reaches perhaps its greatest fulfillment in the verses that deal with clothing. Ballads turn everything they treat into visual images, including topics that normally would be more closely related to other senses. A ballad, more regularly than any other literary

genre, insists on translating its content into visual terms before offering it
to the ears of the audience. The analysis of the references to clothing dis-
closed that not only concepts such as wealth or status, which quite ordinarily find their expression or confirmation in a certain type or quality of
dress, but also psychological processes are rendered visible by color and
fabric, or the offering, giving, receiving, refusing, wearing, changing, and
flaunting of clothes.

Needless to say, a person's emotions often become visible also in reality,
but it happens through his facial expression, posture, or movements. In
ballads, however, visual images have some peculiar characteristics. While
much of the style and structure of ballads brings to mind a theater with a
small stage—the presence of few actors at one time, avoidance of mass
spectacles, scarcity of scenery, abrupt transitions, and, of course, the use
of clothing to identify the characters—there exists also a striking similarity
to the tableaux (as in Cervantes's *Retablo de las maravillas*), known to
have been used in various forms by itinerant singers (for example, the
Bänkelsänger) as visual aids to their presentation. Most popular ballads
can be indeed quite easily broken down to a series of still frames, in the
same manner as biblical stories were depicted on large altarpieces, or in the
manner of today's comic strips, to which some of the tableaux must have
borne great resemblance.[26] This would explain also why the balladist
paints his picture with broad strokes. Of a person's head, he fixes most often the color of the hair; of the overall appearance, he usually chooses to
describe the clothing. He speaks as if he were unable to draw the lines of a
beautiful face or to trace changes in its expression, or—and this is probably closer to the truth—as if a considerable number of his audience were
standing at some distance, where they cannot see fine detail, an audience
like that of a street singer who has climbed on a bench and points to a tableau illustrating his narration, so that even latecomers in the last row,
where some of the words may escape them, are able to follow the story.
This contingency would justify the way persons in ballads show not only
their identity and status but also their feelings by means of their dress.

This is not to say that all ballads were necessarily sung with the support
of actors, mimes, or a tableau, but it does seem probable that singers
either consciously or subconsciously adjusted their style to some form of
visual presentation that precluded continuous or subtle movements and
fine shading, requiring a series of images that revealed the development of
the plot through conspicuous changes, bold colors, and strong contrasts.

These self-imposed restrictions must be largely held accountable for the seeming poverty of ballad imagery, mentioned at the beginning of this chapter. Certain few images—clothing being one of the foremost—comply with such visual limitations more readily than a great many others, and the balladist adapts, therefore, those favorites to an innumerable variety of concepts.

5

A Buffer for a Taboo

Combing

One of the problems that the balladist faces—and successfully solves—is the treatment of the taboo. Certain forms of the hunt allowed the singer to introduce non-Christian elements into the scene without naming any members of the pagan supernatural realm. Another type of hunt paraphrased the man's conquest of a girl. The praise of clothing stood for the praise of the body that it covered; many different motifs involving clothes conveyed other sexual taboos, such as seduction, promiscuity, incest, or adultery. Of all symbolic acts, however, combing is probably the favorite one for expressing sexuality and sometimes also for dealing with the pagan world. Though combing and clothing may circumscribe some of the same taboos, the obvious tactile sensuality of combing, besides being less burdened with the associations with wealth that tended to dominate the motifs involving clothes, make it a more concentrated and more powerful symbol for themes related to the libido.

Prior's observation that "the Scandinavians seem to have thought more of their ladies' hair than of any other feature" (1:255) can easily be verified in a vast number of Danish ballads in his anthology, but suffers from an unnecessary geographic limitation. One may safely say that in describing physical beauty the eye of the European balladist tends to focus on hair. To denote the beauty of a girl by means of praising her hair—usually blond or golden—is an obvious synecdochic process. A simple mention of hair, however, would not completely satisfy the stylistic conventions of balladry, which prefer action to description. Indeed, the most frequent device for drawing attention to the exquisiteness of a girl's hair is by combing, as in *John of Hazelgreen* (Child 293 D):

> Then he's taen out a siller comb,
> Combd down her yellow hair;
> And lookëd in a diamond bright,
> To see if she were fair.

Some degree of action is retained by a verb even in adjectival function in *Alison and Willie* (Child 256):

> "My luve she lives in Lincolnshire,
> I wat she's neither black nor broun,
> But her hair is like the thread o gowd,
> Aye an it waur weel kaimëd doun."

Combing, in these examples, reinforces the synecdochic description of the girl's beauty, and, at the same time, represents a transitional stage to a metonymic process, which omits the hair and mentions only the combing. In Spanish this shift comes very naturally, since in that language a girl does not "comb her hair" but "combs herself." One has to reverse and retrace the steps in these mutations (beautiful girl—beautiful hair—combing beautiful hair—combing) to understand how, for example, the seemingly unemotional verses of *La doncella que va a la guerra* imply a great sacrifice on the part of the girl. We know she is beautiful, since she "se está peinando al sol" as she hears the complaint of her father who has no sons to send to war; by deciding to cut her hair and become a soldier she renounces her feminine beauty and thus her eligibility for marriage, which is implied through her beauty.[1]

Telling examples may be found also in the ubiquitous ballads about the abused daughter-in-law. In a Greek version, a man leaves his wife in the care of his mother and sisters; hardly has he left when they cut her lovely blond hair and send her out to herd mangy sheep and goats (Kind, p. 151). Among the many deprivations this young wife has to suffer, the cutting of her hair suggests an attempt to annul her marriage—an interpretation that is corroborated by the lament of the girl who has her mind set on marriage but is forced to become a nun, and now mourns most of all her hair:

> Me sientan en una silla   y allí me cortan el pelo.
> Pendientes de mis orejas   y anillitos de mis dedos,
> lo que más sentía yo   era mi mata de pelo.[2]

Conversely, Ángela Mesías, who by death escaped a repugnant marriage, is miraculously resuscitated after her lover's return, and, combing her hair, joins the world of the living; she is, in other words, restored to her sexual nature and ready to marry:

> Otro día a la mañana   doña Ángela de Mesías
> peinando sus cabellos   una reina parecía.
> (Cossío and Maza, 1:429)

A similar positive-negative significance is attached to braids and their undoing. To violate a girl's carefully plaited hair is symbolic of violating the girl. The Russian Marfa Petrovichna, who has been captured by three Tatars, cries: "Oh, my unfortunate head! Bitter fate, my dark blond tresses! Last night my mother combed you, combed you, braided you. Well do I know: the three rapacious Tatars will unbraid my dark blond tresses" (Trautmann, p. 396). Likewise the Polish murderer of young girls (related to Halewijn-Ulinger) tells Kasia in the forest to loosen her fair braids, but she protests that her mother did not comb and plait her tresses to have them dragged now over the brambles (Pawlowska, p. 130). A subtle counterpart may be discerned in the *Danza prima* of Asturias: the young man is looking for, and finds, a girl who plaits her hair, expressing beauty, nubility, and maidenhood:

> ¡Ay! busco la blanca niña   ¡ay! busco la niña blanca
> que tiene la voz delgadina,   que tiene la voz delgada;
> la que el cabello tejía,   la que el cabello trenzaba.
> . . . .
> Hallárala una doncella,   hallárala una zagala,
> la qu'el cabello tejía,   la que el cabello trenzaba.
> (Menéndez y Pelayo, 10:79-80)

It follows that in describing preparations for a wedding a ballad singer most likely includes the combing of the bride's hair, as in the Portuguese play-song *La Condessa* (which has many Spanish counterparts, e.g., *Hilito de oro*):

> Lá se vae minha filhinha   vestidinha de cor de rosa
> pentiando seus cabelos   botando banha cheirosa.[3]

The positivistic explanation that a girl, in fact, does comb her hair before her wedding, proves too shallow in the light of the Sephardic *Pesadilla*. There a girl, who has had a dream about the moon, birds, and a golden comb in the middle of the house, is told by her mother that the golden comb is her bridegroom:

> Que un sueño soñaba   de bien y alegría:
> que el peine de oro   en medio de casa,
> y los pajaritos   en sus buraquitos,
> y las palomitas   en sus ventanitas,
> y el lunar entero   en las escaleras

y la media luna . . . —Ésa es tu suegra;
el lunar entero   ése es tu suegro,
y los pajaritos   son tus cuñaditos,
y las palomitas   son tus cuñaditas,
y el peine de oro   ése es tu novio.

(Larrea, 2:114-15)

That in ballads combing functions mainly as a symbol, rather than as the documentation of a custom, comes forth very clearly also in *La lavandera*:

Yo me levantara, madre,   mañanica de Sant Juan;
vide estar una doncella   ribericas de la mar;
sola lava y sola tuerce,   sola tiende en un rosal;
mientras los paños s'enjugan,   dice la niña un cantar:
"¿Dó los mis amores, dó los,   dónde los iré a buscar?"
Mar abajo, mar arriba,   diciendo iba un cantar,
peine de oro en las sus manos   y sus cabellos peinar:
"¿Dígasme tú, el marinero,   que Dios te guarde de mal,
si los viste a mis amores,   si los viste allá pasar?"[4]

The verses about combing have no logical connection to the scene—a young girl washing clothes on the seashore. But their preservation in this concise ballad is far from accidental: their function is to paraphrase and to introduce the girl's question, "Have you seen my love?"

Happy expectation and crushed hope are contrasted by means of combing in two consecutive stanzas of *Fair Margaret and Sweet William* (Child 74 B):

Lady Margaret at her bower window,
   Combing of her hair,
She saw Sweet William and his brown bride
   Unto the church repair.

Down she cast her iv'ry comb,
   And up she tossd her hair,
She went out from her bowr alive,
   But never so more came there.

In a similar story (Child 73 A), Fair Annet, preparing to go to Lord Thomas's wedding to his nut-brown bride, makes a last, desperate, effort:

"My maides, gae to my dressing-roome,
   And dress to me my hair;

> Whaireir yee laid a plait before,
> See yee lay ten times mair.''

Combing figures again prominently in the Sephardic lament of a disappointed bride, whom God made beautiful, yet provided only an old useless husband:

> Dió del sielo, Dió del sielo   que es padre de la piadad,
> me dates cabeyo rubio   para peinar y transar,
> me dates cara hermosa   como rosa en el rosal,
> ....
> me dates marido viejo,   viejo era y de antigüedad;
> para subirse a la cama   no se puede menear.[5]

Also many fairies show by combing that they are on the lookout for a human mate. The *korrigan* who demands marriage from Count Nann is combing her long, blond hair with a golden comb, and La Villemarqué explains in this connection that the *korrigan* want to regenerate their race and, therefore, seek union with humans.[6] In the Faroese ballad of similar content, the elf comes out of an elf-house, braiding her hair, and invites Olaf to dance. His reply leaves no doubt as to the meaning of the braiding: ''You need not braid your hair for me, I have not come a-wooing'' (Child, 1:375). The combing of the *infantina encantada* blends the characteristics of a marriage-minded fairy and of a human girl waiting for love (see p. 33). A version of *El caballero burlado* that has attracted the beginning of *La infantina encantada* shows the girl combing her hair with a golden comb and illuminating the whole mountain with each parting of her hair:

> Con peines d'oro en la mano,   conque los cabellos guía:
> cada vez que los guiaba   el monte resplandecía.[7]

Sometimes the tree she sits in is of gold and silver, and the hair of the infanta covers it entirely:

> La raíz es de oro   y las hojas de plata fina:
> en el pimpollo más alto   vido estar a una infantita:
> cabello de su cabeza   todo aquel roble cubría.[8]

There is nothing irregular in the coincidence of the infanta's combing and the habitual activities of fairies; this transfer of behavior from victor to victim has a parallel in the folklore of Asturias. The *xanas*, who are believed to have powers to enchant people, come to the entrance of their caves, either to do their sewing with golden scissors or to comb their hair with a golden comb. They turn the girls kidnapped by them into beautiful *xanas,* who sit at the entrance of their caves waiting for somebody to disenchant them. In the manner of legitimate *xanas,* these girls also use golden scissors in sewing.[9]

Mermaids, too, can be seen combing, such as the one whose appearance with comb and glass precedes the shipwreck in a British ballad (Child 289):

> Last Easter day, in the morning fair,
> We was not far from land,
> Where we spied a mermaid on the rock,
> With comb and glass in hand.

Also the Finnish water sprites (Spirits of Goldeneye), attracted by Väinämöinen's harp, "were smoothing down their tresses, brushing their locks, with a silver-tipped brush, with a gold brush" (*Kalevala,* poem 41). The extraordinary attention that fairy folk pay their hair, and their possession of golden combs, give combing a connotation of supernatural workings even in cases where the comber belongs to the human species. In the context of ballads, combing is an act of magic, which in the hands of the innocent or the unwise may have powers beyond the intentions of the comber.

Since Spain has fused numerous folk beliefs with stories of Christian personages, it is not surprising to find combing motifs similar to those attached to fairies and mermaids in the *romances a lo divino.* Thus in *La romera* the king is taken with a finely dressed pilgrim who passes through town; his search party finds her combing her hair with gold and silver combs in a poplar grove—a motif that combines feminine attraction and the mysterious powers of a fairy:

> La han encontrado peinando   debajo de una alameda,
> con peines de oro y plata   los sus cabellos los peina.[10]

Both the forest setting and her activity are an appropriate preparation for the imminent transition from the human, everyday, world into the supernatural and marvelous: the pilgrim reveals that she is the mother of God.

As on many other occasions, Prior's comment about combing is correct but somewhat cursory: he finds that the practice "as the occupation of

ladies in leisure moments is as common in Spanish as in Northern ballads"
(3:148). When a wife is waiting for her absent husband, her combing
means much more than a filling of idle hours. For example, the denouement of *La viuda fiel* (*La vuelta del marido*) shows that the wife is waiting
faithfully and lovingly, adamant in refusing anyone else's attentions even
after receiving the false news of her husband's death, as she is combing her
hair:

> Estándome yo peinando   en mi gabinete nuevo,
> vi venir a un caballero   todo vestido de negro.
> Yo me acerqué a preguntarle   como mujer de Laredo:
> —Dígame usted, caballero,   si viene usted de la guerra.
> (Cossío and Maza, 1:202)

A Sephardic version of this *romance* places the lady in a gold and ivory
tree and gives her an ivory comb, reminiscent of *La infantina encantada*,
thus lending her the aura of a woman under a spell who needs to be re-
leased—in this case by her own husband:

> Arboleda, arboleda,   arboleda tan gentil,
> la raíz tiene de oro,   y la rama de marfil
> en la ramica más chica   está la dama tan gentil
> peinándose sus cabellos   con un peine de marfil.
> (Menéndez Pidal, "Romancero judío-español," no. 58)

The comber may also be a wife in acute distress. Escrivana, in a Catalan
romance, is waiting for rescue from Moorish captivity, combing her hair
with combs of silver and gold:

> El primé castell que trova   es del moro Xalandrí,
> allí veu l'Escrivaneta   la veu que 's pentina allí,
> la pinteta n' es de plata   l' escarpidó n' es d' or fi.
> (Milá, p. 158)

In some Portuguese versions of *Gaiferos,* Melisenda—likewise abducted
by a Moor—is combing her hair (in one variant with a golden comb) while
she is anxiously waiting for her liberator (see Menéndez Pidal, *Romancero
hispánico,* 1:288).

Light from a different angle is thrown on the equation "comb-
ing = waiting" by *Blanca Niña* or *La esposa infiel* (*Prim.* 136). A lie in a
folk ballad is not spoken without a purpose; the purpose of the unfaithful

wife is to convince her husband that she has been longingly waiting for him. Thus, when he returns unexpectedly, she lies to him that she has been combing her hair:

> —Señor, peino mis cabellos,   péinolos con gran dolor,
> que me dejéis a mí sola   y a los montes os vais vos.

In asserting that finery in Scottish ballads "is associated with folly, pride, and death; it is Vanity," John Speirs includes *Sir Patrick Spens* (Child 58 A):[11]

> O lang, lang may the ladies stand,
> Wi thair gold kems in their hair,
> Waiting for thair ain deir lords,
> For they'll se thame na mair.

There may well be some reproof for vanity in *Sir Patrick Spens,* but considering some of the other variants, such as 58 B, where the ladies stand with tears blinding their eyes and with their babies in their hands, the main emphasis appears to be on waiting—in this case, waiting in vain, since the lords have drowned. Another variant (58 F) establishes the equivalency combing = waiting cleary enough:

> Our ladies may stand upon the sand,
> Kembing down their yellow hair,
> But they will neer see Skipper Patrick's ship
> Come sailing in nae mair.

Speirs's other example, however, *Proud Lady Margaret* (Child 47), bears out his interpretation of moral censure. Margaret "was a rich ladye,/An vain as vain coud be. . . . She spent her time frae morning till night/Adorning her fair bodye." She is combing her yellow hair when her dead brother, who cannot rest in his grave because of her pride, comes to chide her:

> He got her in her stately ha,
> Kaimin her yellow hair,
> He left her on her sick sick bed,
> Sheding the saut saut tear.

Also in other countries, combing is often a sign of vanity and frivolity.

A Lithuanian song warns a young man not to marry a rich girl, since she would not work but only comb her hair and look in a mirror. A French girl refuses to come home after staying three days with three dragoons, since they do all the housework, and she can spend her time doing up her blond hair. In a Piedmontese ballad, Giordanina, who combs her golden hair on the seashore, is giddy and flirtatious; when her golden earrings fall into the sea, she promises a passing young man 200 lire and a kiss for retrieving them.[12] In a Catalan *romance* about the penitence of Mary Magdalen, combing expresses her worldliness before her conversion. Martha comes from Mass and finds Magdalen combing her hair with a golden comb; Martha asks whether she has been to Mass; Magdalen replies that she has not, nor has she planned to go (Doncieux, p. 146).

In a different category of ballads, more frequent in the *Romancero,* the sexual attraction conveyed through combing may render a girl vulnerable to an unsanctioned suit, as in *La dama de Aragón*:

> A Aragó n'hi ha una dama   que es bonica com un sol;
> té la cabellera rossa: li arriba fins als talons.
> . . . .
> Sa mare la pentinava   amb una pinteta d'or;
> sa tia los hi esclaria   los cabells de dos en dos.
> Cada cabell una perla,   cada perla un anell d'or.

Her brother remarks admiringly that he would marry her if they were not brother and sister:

> Son germà se la mirava   amb un ull tot amorós,
> —No fossim germans, María,   nos casariem tots dos.[13]

While here the incest motif is somewhat vague, it forms the main theme of *Delgadina* and *Silvana*. Sephardic versions of both *romances* begin with identical verses: the princess is unwittingly attracting the eye of her father by combing her hair with a golden comb:

> Estábase la Silvana   en silla de oro sentada,
> peine de oro en la su mano   los sus cabellos peinaba.
> Por ahí pasó el rey su padre   que de ella se enamorara.
> (Larrea, 1:336)

Another case of breaking a taboo is *El sacrílego,* in which a priest falls in love with a little girl. After her parents' death, he finds her combing her hair in the sunshine:

> Un día por la mañana   se salió a peinar al sol,
> los peines eran de plata,   de acero el escarpidor;
> pasó por allí el mal cura,   pasó por allí el traidor.
> —Pepina, la mi Pepina,   dame de tu pecho amor.
> (Cossío and Maza, 1:453)

The defenseless girl is forced to accompany the priest, who causes her death. Again, the charm of a girl combing her hair incites the abductor in the Sephardic fairy-tale fantasy, *El culebro raptor,* in which the infanta is carried away by a dragon-like reptile:

> Estábase allí la infanta   en silla de oro sentada,
> peine de oro en la su mano   rubios cabellos peinaba.
> Por allí pasó el culebro   que de ella se enamorara.
> (Menéndez Pidal, "Romancero
> judío-español," no. 93)

The countess in the Majorcan *Les dues Dianes* is courted under similar circumstances by a serpent, who introduces himself as an enchanted king:

> Estava la gentil dama   a l'ombra d'una murtera,
> amb una pinteta d'or   pentinaut sa cabeiera;
> en l'altra mà té un mirai   per mirar sa cara bella.
> Quan se va haver pentinat   a su-baix d'una font fresca
> ella sent una remor   i fixa sus uis en terra;
> veu venir una serpent,   que aixeca el cap i el redreça.[14]

The mirror in line 3 adds to the characterization of the comber a nuance, found also in the following examples. A Swedish version of the Scandinavian songs about Solfot (Solfager, Suol-far) describes her as looking at her face in the water and saying: "God help me for my beauty! Surely I shall come to a strange land." She needs but comb her hair out-of-doors, and Ormeking tricks her away; her husband goes on a search and finds her—combing her hair out-of-doors (Child, 5:7). Another Swedish ballad, also retold by Child (4:440), begins in a very similar way: "Fru Malin is combing her hair *al fresco,* when a suitor enters her premises. He remarks that a crown would sit well on her head." Fru Malin soon falls for the glib tongue of the stranger; as they leave together, the horse stumbles on a bridge, she falls into the river, and is done for. Fru Malin's head was turned by sophisticated courtship and probably by the not-quite-human nature of her suitor, but she also seems easy prey. Each of the three combing wives displays a touch of unbecoming and provocative vanity, which makes them different from the innocent victims of uninvited observers in earlier quoted songs. Fru Malin was susceptible to flattery; Solfot and the Majorcan countess admired the reflections of their own faces.

While the married ladies in the foregoing ballads can be perhaps classified as merely abduction-prone, incipient infidelity is obvious in the attitude of the wife in the introductory verses of *La esposa infiel*:

> Mañanita, mañanita,   mañanita e San Simón,
> estaba una señorita   sentadita 'n su balcón,
> muy peinada y muy lavada,   los ojitos d'arrebol.
> (Menéndez y Pelayo, 10:180)

Here and in another Andalusian variant the lady is already combed and made up; in the same ballad from Santander (four out of ten variants given by Cossío and Maza), she is combing her hair on the balcony or at the window:

> Estando una señorita   peinándose en el balcón,
> pasó por allí un soldado   de buena y mala intención.
> —Señorita, señorita,   con usted durmiera yo.
> —Suba, suba el caballero,   dormirá una noche o dos.
> (Cossío and Maza, 1:220)

In a Sephardic version of *El pastor lindo*, the lady at the window surpasses the unfaithful wife of the preceding songs in lasciviousness by taking the initiative and praising her own charms (including her hair), in order to seduce an untractable shepherd. She is introduced at the beginning of the ballad in a manner strongly reminiscent of the *romance* of the unfaithful wife:

> En la siudad de Venesya   avía una ermoza dama,
> se peynava i se afeytava   en la ventana se asentava.[15]

The combing in the last few ballads would mean to the audience something different from the combing in the songs about faithfully waiting wives or dreamy-eyed young girls. Those who know the story beforehand can, of course, anticipate the significance of the combing, but even the uninitiated are given clues to the character of the lady and the purpose of her comb-ing. Thus, in the two Andalusian variants of *La esposa infiel* and in the Se-phardic *Pastor lindo,* the pleasure-minded woman uses for attraction not only her hairdo, but also cosmetics ("los ojitos d'arrebol," or "su poquito de arrebol," in *La esposa infiel*; "se peynava i se afeytava" in *El pastor lindo*).[16] Self-contemplation in a mirror (or its equivalent) by the Majorcan lady in *Les dues Dianes* or by the Scandinavian Solfot, above, invites trou-ble, to say the least. In *Landarico* and its Sephardic equivalent, *Andarleto,* the mirror and the lady's self-admiration are coupled with unbraided hair—a symbol implying loss of chastity, as seen earlier in this chapter. In-deed, the sinister foreboding is borne out in the ballad. The king finds the queen with her hair loose, looking in a mirror ("Mirándose está a un espejo,   el cabello destrenzado"); in the Sephardic version she is praising God for having created her so beautiful. It turns out that she has a lover of long standing; upon learning that the king knows about the affair, she has him murdered.[17]

In several of the foregoing examples the woman's immoral character was indicated by her combing at the window (or on a balcony, which in Spain would mean the same place). Combing her hair at the window is also the practice of the predatory Gayarda, who holds a continual spider's feast:

> Estándose la Gayarda   en su ventana dorida
> peinando su pelo negro   que paez seda torcida,
> vio un bizarro caballero   venir por la calle arriba.
> —Venga, venga el caballero,   venga a ver la mi montisa;
> comerán pan de lo blanco   vino tinto de Castilla.[18]

She seduces men for her pleasure, which ends in murder, and decorates her dwelling with as many as a hundred heads.

While women's hair is their most frequently mentioned feature in bal-lads and they comb it without regard to nationality, men do not receive equal treatment in all countries. Danish *viser* and Russian *byliny* swarm with men who have yellow curls (in Russia often compared to pearls), and occasionally a Scottish lad—Young Bekie, Glenkindie, Willie o Wins-bury—is similarly distinguished. But it is a rare case indeed where we see a man combing his hair, as, for example, Child Maurice, who "according to the unvarying traditions of the country, was remarkable for the extreme

length and loveliness of his yellow hair" (Child, 2:264, quoting Mother-
well), and who in the ballad "tooke his siluer combe in his hand,/To
kembe his yellow lockes" (Child 83).

The *Romancero* omits hair in nearly all physical descriptions of young
men (*canas* are sometimes mentioned, but appear to refer mainly to the
beard). In *Las señas del esposo*—an imported ballad, according to
Menéndez Pidal (*Romancero hispánico*, 1:318)—the husband is sometimes
remembered as "blanco, rubio y colorado," but there are also many variants in which the wife says only that he is fair and young, and then proceeds to describe his fine clothing and his superior skills. An isolated
comber is Vergilios (*Prim.* 111), who laments the length of his stay in the
dungeon:

> —Señor, peino mis cabellos,   y las mis barbas también:
> Aquí me fueron nacidas,   aquí me han de encanecer;
> que hoy se cumplen siete años   que me mandaste prender.

Another is Frei João, who prepares himself to court a married woman;
hence his combing is a sign of corruption, as it was in many characteriza-
tions of unfaithful wives:

> Erguera-se Frei João   uma manhã de geada
> penteando o seu cabello,   tocando sua guitarra,
> foi á porta da Morena,   da Morena mal casada.
> (Braga, *Açoriano,* p. 378)

One could, perhaps, assume that combing meant little to Spanish men.
However, the sensuality so conspicuous in verses dealing with women can
be found in the *Romancero,* as well as in ballads of other countries, in a
special variety of combing that reveals the extent of the joys it held for a
man. In a *romance* that (very freely) retells the judgment of Paris, the hero
falls asleep in a sensually ideal landscape—among lilies, roses, and sweetly
singing nightingales. Three ladies, who later turn out to be goddesses, sur-
round him. Dressed in gold, silk, pearls, and precious stones, they render
Paris personal services; one combs his hair, another fans him, and the
third mops his brow:

> La una le peina el cabello,   la otra aire le hacía,
> la otra le coge el sudor   que de su rostro salía.
> (*Cancionero de romances, sin año,* fol. 195)

The sensual revelry that surrounds this kind of combing is elaborated also in the secret meeting of an adulterous wife and her lover in *La infanticida*:

> Ella lo peina y lo lava,   y en su regazo lo acuesta,
> y le daba del buen pan,   del que tenía pa ella,
> y le daba del buen vino,   del bueno de su bodega.
>   (*La flor de la marañuela,* 2:40)

In the Sephardic *Repulsa y compasión,* the girl relents after pushing a seducer into the sea, throws him her braids to pull him out, and comforts him by, among other things, combing his hair with an ivory comb:

> Le lavé sus pies y manos   con el agua de azahar;
> le peiné los sus cabellos   con un peine de marfil.
>   (Larrea, 2:60)

Few as they are in Spanish ballads, these descriptions of a hedonistic heaven, where combing plays a prominent part, surpass by far the corresponding passages in ballads of other countries. In Denmark, the act seems quite conventional, as "Knight Stig at court an office bare,/And maids and ladies brush'd his hair" (DgF 76, trans. Prior, 2:339). When Germand Gladensvend (DgF 33) has to surrender to a ravenous monster, Adelutz combs his hair in a last, tearful farewell. Else does the same for Aage, who died on their wedding night and returns as a revenant (DgF 90). Combing a dead lover's hair becomes part of a primitive rite in *The Braes o Yarrow* (Child 214):

> She kissed his cheek, she kaimd his hair
> As oft she did before, O;
> She drank the red blood frae him ran,
> On the dowy houms o Yarrow.

The sexes are reversed in a few exceptional cases where combing represents a man's love:

> "Or who will comb my bony head
> With the red river comb;
> Or who will be my bairn's father
> Ere Gregory he come home?"
> (*The Lass of Roch Royal,* Child 76)

In a version of *La condesita,* the disguised countess points out her features to her long-lost husband and reminds him that he used to comb her blond hair: "Que tienes tu cara bella   que solías besar,/y tienes tu pelo rubio   que tú solías peinar" (*Romancero tradicional,* 4:124). Granted that in a number of other ballads the chief motives for combing appear to be tenderness and compassion between relatives, the pleasure derived from being combed would still be classified as sexual pleasure, if Freudian terms are applied.[19]

The erotic objective is quite pronounced in *Allison Gross* (Child 35)— the tale of a youth who is harassed by the amorous pursuit of "the ugliest witch in the north country": "She stroaked my head, and she kembed my hair,/An she set me down saftly on her knee." Also Burd Isabel (Child 257) resorts to combing in her attempt to set the obstinate Earl Patrick's mind on marriage.

At the same time, there is a strong likelihood that in the love scenes of early ballads not combing but lousing was the prevalent motif. In English, the word has mainly lapsed from current use. It cannot be replaced with the "delousing" of modern refugee camps, since the new word lacks the leisure and the caress—in short, the whole complex of emotional and sensual connotations of "lousing." The need for comment has been recognized by editors of folk ballad collections such as the comprehensive *Deutsche Volkslieder,* which calls it "das Lausen, ein mittelalterlich häufig geübter Liebesdienst" (2:96). The very well chosen word *Liebesdienst* is not easily translatable. It is a "kindly office," but is more accurately circumscribed by its component parts: a service rendered because of love and with love. During the Victorian era, critics shied away from direct terminology, even in discussing old ballads. Child quotes Dozon ("cette action, si peu séante pour nous") and speaks of "the most homely of services" or "the unromantic service" (1:27, 37), although his own examples give the lie to the last phrase: lousing occurs in folktales as a service by young girls to their lovers, by abducted princesses to dragons, by a lady to Saint George (who liberated her from the dragon), and was requested also by a dead man recalled to the earth by his mistress (Child, 1:487).

The Spanish *Cautivo,* which in its longer versions elaborates the love affair between a Moorish woman and a Christian captive,[20] in the laconic sixteenth-century text (*Prim.* 131) condenses the love story into a few verses:

> Pero plugo a Dios del cielo   que tenía el ama buena:
> cuando el moro se iba a caza   quitábame la cadena,
> y echárame en su regazo,   y espulgóme la cabeza;
> por un placer que le hice   otro muy mayor me hiciera;
> diérame los cien doblones   y enviárame a mi tierra;
> y así plugo a Dios del cielo   que en salvo me pusiera.

In early ballads such as this, lousing seems to be the symbol of an intense intimacy, either just short of, or perhaps even including, sexual union. For laying his head in an unwilling partner's lap, many a man pays dearly, as does the Moorish king whose head the captive Juliana cuts off with a sharp knife:

> El rey, como era chiquito,   en su halda se echó a espulgare;
> tomó navajita aguda,   y degollóle por detrase.[21]

In the ballads of the German *Ulinger* series, the killer of girls often requests the loving service when he tells his victim to sit down with him on his cloak:

> Er breit sein Mantel in das Graß
> er bat sie, das sie zu jhm saß;
> Er sprach, sie solt jhm lausen,
> sein gelbes Har zerzausen.
> (*Deutsche Volkslieder*, 2:72)

Neither this girl nor, in like situations, the Hungarian Anna Molnár and Kate Ban are quite ready to rid themselves of the uncanny swains,[22] but the Danish Venelil makes good use of lovers' etiquette: with his head on her lap, Wulfstan falls asleep; she ties him up, wakes him, and kills him with his own sword (DgF 183). While the motif of lousing occurs in most Scandinavian ballads in this group, few of them elaborate the girl's plotting as clearly as a version of *Lady Isabel and the Elf-Knight* (Child 4 A):

> "O sit down a while, lay your head on my knee,
> That we may hae some rest before that I die."
>
> She stroak'd him sae fast, the nearer he did creep,
> Wi a sma charm she lulld hin fast asleep.

Lady Isabel ties up the fiend and kills him with his own dagger, but without the courtesy of waking him first. In the last ballads, the soporific effect is obviously not due just to the gentle hand that strokes the hair, but to related magic practices. The handling of the man's hair makes him, who originally wielded the stronger weapons, vulnerable to the "small charm." One may suspect that vestiges of witchcraft lurk also behind other ballads that show a girl grooming a man's hair.

The transition in ballad language from lousing to combing must have come about through a refinement of diction, and perhaps even more, through a change in actual custom. It is significant that lousing has remained in ballads about villains such as Ulinger and his counterparts, while poems about love in courtly circles required a more genteel act.

The exquisite enjoyment either expected or promised by those who comb their own hair, and delivered by those who render the service to others, makes combing an essential ingredient in vows of renunciation, which are found in both Spanish and British ballads, though with certain national differences.

In his Lenten penitence, a pious Spanish king, besides sleeping on a chair with a stone for a pillow, neither grooms his beard nor combs his hair:

> Desde el miércoles corvillo   hasta el jueves de la Cena,
> que el rey no hizo la barba   ni peinó la su cabeza.
> *(Prim.* 64)

This king was known for his saintly life (he was later canonized), and by all available indications, his penance was not done for any particular sin, but as an accumulation of merit on the way to glory; in other words, it was a preparatory, rather than a retrospective, discipline. Similar timing may be observed in *Marqués de Mantua (Prim.* 165), where the marquis promises not to comb his grey hair, cut his beard, and so forth, until he has avenged his nephew's death or died in the endeavor:

> —Juro por Dios poderoso   por Santa María su Madre,
> y al santo Sacramento   que aquí suelen celebrar,
> de nunca peinar mis canas   ni las mis barbas cortar;
> de no vestir otras ropas,   ni renovar mi calzar;
> de no entrar en poblado,   ni las armas me quitar,
> si no fuere una hora   para mi cuerpo limpiar;

> de no comer a manteles,   ni a mesa me asentar,
> fasta matar a Carloto   por justicia o pelear,
> o morir en la demanda,   manteniendo la verdad.

Likewise Count Dirlos (*Prim*. 164) refuses to cut beard or hair during his fifteen-year campaign in the land of the Moors:

> Las barbas y los cabellos   nunca los quiso afeitar;
> tiénelos fasta la cinta,   fasta la cinta, y aun más:
> la cara mucho quemada   del mucho sol y del aire,
> con el gesto demudado   muy fiero y espantable.

His waist-long hair enables him to return incognito, and not even his wife recognizes him until he pulls it back from his face. But he still will not give up his "savage looks," since it turns out that he is about to be defrauded of both wife and lands; only after receiving satisfaction for his grievance does he finally trim his beard and hair. Count Dirlos obeys, in fact, the conventions of his social position since several of the aforementioned deprivations used to be compulsory for a knight who had not avenged an injury. Montesinos, after being insulted by Oliveros, renounces, among other things, eating from a tablecloth and cropping his beard (*Prim*. 177a), and the Cid, in the epic poem, vows not to let scissors enter his beard, because King Alfonso has banished him upon a false denunciation.[23]

The corresponding custom in British ballads, though similar in wording, is practiced by women.[24] After May Margaret's brothers have killed her lover (*Clerk Saunders,* Child 69 D), she vows:

> "And I will do for my love's sake
>   What many ladies would not do;
> Seven years shall come and go
>   Before I wear stocking or shoe.
>
> "There'll neer a shirt go on my back,
>   There'll neer a kame go in my hair,
> There'll never coal nor candle-light
>   Shine in my bower nae mair."

In *Lord Livingston* (Child 262), the lady makes such vows after the lord is slain in a fight with Seaton; in *Bonny Bee Hom* (Child 92), "I never loved a love but ane,/And now he's gone away." In *Jamie Douglas* (Child 204

E), the lady has been slandered and, as a consequence, abandoned by her husband; she rejects her father's suggestion to write a bill of divorce and get her a "better lord." So far, it seems that the ladies, in losing their men, have lost all reason for caring for their looks and become insensitive to creature comforts, since they also renounce coal and candlelight, washing their faces, wearing gloves, stockings, and clean shirts, and promise to wear dowy black. But *The Coble o Cargill* and *Little Musgrave and Lady Barnard* (Child 242, 81 L) add another facet: in the former the jealous lass of Balathy who makes the vows has sunk the boat of the two-timing butler of Stobhall; in the latter, the lord has killed his wife and her lover and now regrets the rash deed (an exceptional case among British ballads in that the vows are made by a man). Thus the renunciation of combing and of other similar habits is not just an act of mourning but, at times, also of penance.

Besides the sex of the person likely to pronounce the vows, there is another national difference. The Spanish context shows the vows as a part of the aggressive movement; they are involved in action and lead to action; they appear in ballads at a moment when the plot is on an upswing, often after the initial conflict. The British ballads, in contrast, usually have already reached the climax and the tragic denouement before the renunciation is made. Thus the vows represent a reverberation of the passion of crime or, more often, of the shock of bereavement, uttered in a state of resignation and suffering. In both countries, however, the self-imposed abstentions appear to have a significance that goes beyond mere indifference to niceties at a time of grief or stress. Indeed, it is almost as if the comb were sacrificed as an object dear to the supplicant, who expects, in turn, absolution and grace. Within the ascetic content of the vows, to go unkempt belongs to a special moral category. While some other details have specific reference to poverty, the renunciation of combing—in the light of its unmistakable sexual emphasis—must be considered tantamount to a vow of chastity.

6

A CASE OF
VESTED INTEREST

Magic Music

The person of the singer seldom enters the text of a ballad. Now and then he may exhort the audience to pay attention to a particularly pertinent line, but even this is intended to benefit the listener more than the singer. Nevertheless, there are some well-known motifs involving music or singing in which the balladist doubtless has a personal, practical interest. I propose to explore two *romances*, with the support of many other ballads, in order to show a certain fallacy in a familiar interpretation of the motif of magic music, and, then, to attempt a redefinition of this and other related motifs.

Two singers in the Hispanic *Romancero* have been intermittently suspected of not belonging to the human race. One is the nameless sailor in the *Romance del Infante Arnaldos*; the other is a man of many names, of which Conde Olinos is probably the best known.

Critics such as Entwistle and Spitzer who have tried to establish family trees for those two persons point out that the names of the protagonists incriminate the characters in question: "Olinos" resembles "Halewijn" and "Ulinger"—Continental relatives of the British elf-knight; "Arnaldos" may have a connection with the Wild Host.[1] The principal cause for suspicion appears to lie, however, in the fact that the singing of both the skipper and Olinos proves much too effective to have originated in a mere human being. The songs have two separate effects. One pertains to the narrative: the princess in one *romance* and Arnaldos in the other are drawn to the respective singers. The second effect is a ballad commonplace, which at times is dismissed as such but at others is used as evidence of supernatural powers of the singer: wind and water calm down, birds and fish stop in their course, other creatures and things behave in an abnormal manner. Ramón Menéndez Pidal, who sees nothing supernatural in the long and, in his opinion, early version of *Infante Arnaldos,* maintains that the original story of adventure and recognition received a supernatural component only by the addition of the commonplace of the power of song:

> Marinero que la manda   diciendo viene un cantar
> que la mar facía en calma   los vientos hace amainar,
> los peces que andan 'nel hondo   arriba los hace andar,
> las aves que andan volando   en el mástel las face posar.
>
> (Prim. 153)

Leo Spitzer, while disagreeing with Menéndez Pidal about the absence of the supernatural in the original *romance*, dwells on the association of song with the nonhuman character of a number of ballad personages, and thus supports his hypothesis that the skipper was an *Elementargeist*.

For the erudite critic it is relatively easy to trace back a great many fictional characters to supernatural prototypes. Whenever such tracing reaches as far as the mythological stages of a motif, it is likely to connect with a god or demigod. Orpheus, who commanded most of the uses of music that will interest us in the present context, was the son of Apollo; with that in mind, all music may be viewed a priori as supernatural. Quite a different problem is the identity of singing characters in the existent texts of traditional ballads at the time of the active life of such texts. Is there anything in those texts themselves that would suggest the supernatural to an unlettered audience? As W. M. Hart observes, the popular ballad does not give special treatment to ghosts and supernatural beings, and, thus, the supernatural element readily disappears. Gerould, in speaking of a group of ballads that is of specific interest in this study, says that "there can be no question that the malevolent lover in *Lady Isabel and the Elf-Knight* was a supernatural being from the beginning," but adds that "neither in the British versions of the ballad nor in their Continental relatives is the nature of the creature made altogether clear—obviously because it has not been clear, for centuries at least, to those who have sung about it."[2]

While the balladry of northern Europe retains many elements that are unmistakably supernatural, the *Romancero* has dealt with such elements in several devious ways. Sometimes a passage is rationalized; at other times it is suppressed, Christianized, or, in a typically Spanish manner, replaced by lyric motifs that suggest the supernatural without stating it openly. I deal with this problem at length in other chapters, but would like to add here a peculiar case of nonhuman song: in the Canary Islands the *Romance de la infantina* regularly omits the reason for the girl's spending seven years in the forest (enchantment by seven fairies), but, at the same time, elaborates the motif of singing snakes, which creates an atmosphere of mystery and marvel, without making a commitment to pagan beliefs.[3] Thus, the lyric motifs in a *romance* are not necessarily mere ornaments to the narrative but may serve as a seemingly innocuous disguise for a taboo, such as a supernatural, non-Christian, element.

The question here is whether the motif of the power of music does classify the singers in *Infante Arnaldos* and *Conde Olinos* as supernatural beings. Closely connected with this is another question: is there enough justification for relating these singers to the evil breed of Halewijn, Ulinger, and the elf-knight? And, finally, in case the motif of music does not prove to have classifying functions of either kind—then what purpose does it serve?

With no trouble at all one can find in European balladry plenty of non-human creatures who employ music in furthering their evil ends. Scandinavian elf-queens and dwarf-princesses are likely to sit in the forest, playing a golden harp and singing in the hope of attracting young men. Their music customarily arrests bird and beast, or drives the meadow to bloom and the trees to green, (DgF 34, 46). Such elaboration does not appear mandatory, however. It does not accompany, for example, the Breton *korrigan,* though they are known for their beautiful voices. British ballads attach to elfmusic in similar circumstances mainly aphrodisiac qualities: Lady Margaret drops her sewing as she hears "a note in Elmond's wood" and runs off to spend seven years with Hind Etin (Child 41); Lady Isabel hears the elf-knight blowing his horn and exclaims, "If I had yon horn that I hear blawing,/And yon elf-knight to sleep in my bosom" (Child 4 A). We find a similar directness in Continental counterparts of the latter ballad: the Dutch Halewijn sings a song that attracts everybody who hears it; the princess goes with him against the urgent warnings of all members of her family. The German versions of *Ulinger* dwell a trifle longer on the song itself: it resounds in hill and valley, or is made up of "dreierlei Stimmen"—a puzzling quality that has led to many mythological and musicological conjectures. Often enough the girl wishes to learn the song, and the sinister rider promises to teach it to her if she goes along with him.

If the search were to end at this point, the latter detail could be taken as a clinching argument for the inclusion of the sailor, who sets Arnaldos a similar condition, in the host of elvish seducers. The critics who subscribe to this classification readily overlook the fact that Arnaldos and the skipper are of the same sex. Spitzer proffers the argument that ''the lure of the *Elementargeist* is, so to speak, above sex,'' though he fails to cite a convincing parallel (examples do exist both in Iberian and Nordic folklore for the seduction of girls by female elves, or again for the abduction of men— without any lure of song—by such as the Wild Host). A far more serious shortcoming, however, is the fact that the circumstantial evidence for the sailor's kinship to nonhuman seducers is drawn from only one subdivision of the ballads containing the motif of music—the subdivision in which song and music are the prerogative of nonhuman creatures with evil intentions.

In France there are several versions of a folk song known as *La belle se promène* or *L'embarquement de la fille* in which a girl wishes to learn a song from passing sailors. They set the condition that may be expected: she has to embark. In some versions she falls asleep and wakes up crying for her stolen heart (euphemism for lost virginity?); in others, as also in the Piedmontese *Corsaro,* she defends her virtue by committing suicide. In one variant she is tossed into the sea by the sailor.[4] Even if the singing sailors should have supernatural antecedents (as Spitzer maintains), these ballads, in their existing form, stay on a human—one would almost say ''realistic''—plane with their stories of seduction that is either avoided or accomplished. In the latter case the mood in the songs is playful rather than tragic. Still, if a division into heroes and villains must be made, I have to concede that all these sailors would be lumped into the second category.

This derogatory classification is, however, shattered if the singing sailor turns out to be a prince who has come for a bride. This is the case in *El rey marinero,* a Catalan ballad that curiously coincides with some parts of a Sephardic version of *Infante Arnaldos* (Milá, p. 151; cf. Bénichou, *Romancero,* p. 207). After a girl has been invited on board to choose embroidery silk, she falls asleep to the song of the sailor: ''Amb el cant del mariné/s' ha 'dormideta'' (*Arnaldos*: ''Al son de los dulces cantos, el conde dormido se ha''). When she awakens and complains of her hard luck in having become attached to a sailor, he reveals that he is the son of the king of England and has been roving for seven years, looking for her: ''Set anys ha que vaig pel mon,/per vos, donzella'' (the sailor to Arnaldos: ''Siete años hazían, siete, que por ti ando por la mar''). In the Germanic *Kudrunlied* we find a similarly happy union of Hetel and Hilde after Hetel's emissary Horand has enchanted Hilde with his masterful song, which, incidentally, stops birds from singing, forest beasts from grazing, and worms in the grass and fish in the waves from pursuing their course.[5]

One may object, following Spitzer's argument, that any abduction by ship represents the supernatural force of the sea over man, and the song of the abductor is an attribute of this sinister power. But we should also consider such ballads as the Danish *Venderkongens Jomfrurov,* in which Kirsten, abducted with her fourteen companions by the Wendish king, moves with her song both nature and the king's heart:

> Yea, glad were all the little fish
> That swam in sea and flood,
> And glad was every hart and hind
> That played in good greenwood.
>
> And glad were all the men that rowed
> In boats upon the sea,
> And loud he laughed, the King of the Wends,
> For gladder than all was he.
> (DgF 240, trans. Smith-Dampier, p. 287)

The king is persuaded to make Kirsten his queen—the victim enchants the abductor and imposes her will on him. Indeed the balladry of Scandinavia, which, on the one hand, displays an impressive number of singing (and dancing) elf-maidens wishing to snare a human, just as frequently allows a human, by his singing, to subdue a supernatural creature. In the retrieval of a bride from a water spirit, two Orphean motifs are usually combined:

> He played so soft and low,
> No bird moved on the bough.
>
> He played so loud and clear
> 'Twas heard both far and near.
>
> From oaken-tree the bough was torn
> And from the lowing cow the horn.
>
> The bark sprang from the birk
> And the vane from our Lady's kirk.
>
> So strong the spell, so sure the charm,
> He played the bride from Kelpie's arm.
> (DgF 40, trans. Smith-Dampier, p. 106)

Also in the British *Twa Brothers* (Child 49 B), Lady Margaret raises her betrothed temporarily from the dead:

> She put the small pipes to her mouth,
> And she harped both far and near,
> Till she harped the small birds off the briers,
> And her true love out of the grave.

King Orfeo's playing (Child 19) makes the fairy king release Lady Isabel:

> And first he played da notes o noy,
> An dan he played da notes o joy.
>
> An dan he played da göd gabber reel,
> Dat meicht ha made a sick hert hale.

All the foregoing examples should make us realize that singing—even singing that achieves marvelous results—does not classify the singer as either nonhuman or human, "good" or "evil." It is only from the context that we may deduce the characterization in each case; and normally a ballad story guides us quite reliably in the right direction. But what if there is no story to speak of, as in *Infante Arnaldos* in its best-known form? Even if it originally was, as Menéndez Pidal believes, a ballad of adventure—kidnapping and happy reunion—the existence of several truncated texts indicates a circulation of short forms during some period. The question is, What could the truncated *romance* have suggested to those among whom it was current?

For lack of a story, it appears advisable to examine the motifs in the part of the *romance* that precedes the sailor's song:

> ¡Quién hubiese tal ventura   sobre las aguas de mar,
> como hubo el conde Arnaldos   la mañana de San Juan!
> Con un falcón en la mano   la caza iba cazar,
> vio venir una galera   que a tierra quiere llegar.
> Las velas traía de seda,   la ejercia de un cendal.
>
> (*Prim.* 153)

Saint John's Day is in the *Romancero* a day for special events. In some cases, perhaps, "San Juan" has been chosen merely for its convenient assonance, but in others the pre-Christian significance of Midsummer, with its presence of supernatural beings, comes clearly to the fore. There is no need to seek proof outside Spain, as Spitzer does, or even outside the

Romancero. The person of the Virgin in *La flor del agua* is only a thin Christian disguise for the belief that one can find a husband by being the first to skim the water on the morning of Saint John. This is also the time when the devil tempts the drowning sailor in *El marinero.* Maidens and brides are abducted by Moors (a rationalization of hostile spirits?) on Saint John's Day, but also the shores of the sea have a similar significance. The kidnapping of Melchor and Laurencia, and of a girl in the Catalan *Dos hermanos,* takes place on Saint John's Day on the seashore (a combination that can lead also to other startling experiences, as those of the Marquis of Mantua, who is guided by mysterious forces to his dying nephew).[6] The hunt motif, as we have noted, is a Spanish favorite for suggesting an intervention of supernatural powers.

Even though descriptions of ships are rare in the *Romancero,* the fabulous galley that Arnaldos sees has at least one counterpart. The ship of Paris, which arouses the curiosity of Queen Helen with its cargo of silver and gold and thus facilitates her abduction, is, in a Sephardic variant, rigged with sails and ropes of silk and a white crystal rudder (Menéndez y Pelayo, 10:315). This, in turn, brings to mind the ship on which James Harris, the daemon lover, abducts his fickle sweetheart; she could not behold any mariners, "but the sails were o the taffetie,/And the masts o the beaten gold" (Child 243 F).

After this highly suggestive preparation, and the initial verse, "Quién hubiese tal ventura," the broadside and the Sephardic versions of *Infante Arnaldos* are something of a disappointment:

> Marinero que la guía   va diciendo este cantar:
> —Galera, la mi galera,   Dios te me guarde de mal,
> de los peligros del mundo,   de fortunas de la mar,
> de los golfos de León   y estrecho de Gibraltar,
> de las fustas de los moros   que andaban a saltear.[7]

This is the song of a man who is aware of danger and of his own inadequacy—a song equally suitable for primitive man, hoping to influence by the magic of words the powers ordinarily beyond his control, and for the devout, praying to God for protection. What the song is not, however, is the song of an abductor, particularly of a demonic abductor. The reaction of Arnaldos, which in Sephardic versions follows the text of the sailor's song, appears disproportionately intense:

Allí habló el infante Arnaldos,   bien oiréis lo que dirá;
—Por tu vida, el marinero,   vuelve y repite el cantar.
—Quien mi cantar quiere oír   en mi galera ha de entrar.

The powerful combination of introductory motifs leaves little doubt that Arnaldos will board the ship; in Sephardic versions we know for sure that he does. Yet the song that supposedly emanates an irresistible attraction is the weakest part of the poem. Among the well-known European ballads of abduction, and even more broadly, among the ballads that deal with the power of song in diverse situations, this version of *Infante Arnaldos* is anomalous in spelling out the sailor's song.[8] In the majority of such ballads the power of music is conveyed by a description of the results only, and evidently the recasters of *Infante Arnaldos* decided to follow suit, in dropping from the truncated version the words of the sailor's song and substituting a motif that appeared worthier of the tension built up by the introduction and of Arnaldos's response. The adventure that a fabulous ship offered a hunter on the seashore on Saint John's Day had to be more than just a voyage with a skipper who was worried about Moorish pirates and the hazards of navigation. The truncated version leaves the audience guessing as to the nature of the adventure as such, as well as to the contents of the song, and, thus, averts possible disappointment. The verses about the power of the song over waves, wind, fish, and birds, which took the place of the song itself, were nothing novel; they had been used in both traditional and erudite Spanish poetry;[9] but their imaginative force was a match for the introductory passage. The resulting version of the *Romance del Infante Arnaldos* is, in fact, a battery of commonplaces—Saint John's Day, hunt, seashore, fabulous ship, effect of song—none of which by itself, not even the so-called magic song motif, represents unequivocally a supernatural factor, but which together, by interaction and mutual reinforcement, charge the atmosphere with mysterious powers that are capable of manipulating man's fate. Whether or not the singing sailor is of elvish ancestry, the possibility of his being something more than an ordinary seaman is created on the lyric terms of the *Romancero*.

At the same time, possibility must not be confused with proof. In an as yet unknown "complete" version of *Infante Arnaldos,* from which the Sephardic texts are thought to derive, the promise of a supernatural theme may have been borne out by the narrative; but it would be irresponsible to insist that the truncated version retained for the audience over any length of time a supernatural element by virtue of an earlier existence of such an element in the person of the sailor. The supernatural is there only by virtue of insinuation and suggestion; it is not necessarily associated with the sailor in particular.

As to the putative evil character of the sailor, the supporting evidence is meager. Even with regard to the narrative Sephardic version, the controversy between Menéndez Pidal and Spitzer remains unsettled: does the sailor have a dual role as captor-rescuer or are there two different sailors? In the truncated version the sailor does no more than sing and invite Arnaldos to embark. The reason for such an invitation, as was shown earlier, may be either base or noble. The other motif connected with the sailor—the magic effect of the song—is almost as ambiguous. However, it must be noted that while in northern Europe the song of both good and evil creatures may have power over nature, the *Romancero* tends to use it as a sign of approbation. An example is the Portuguese Nativity ballad, *Tres Reis,* where the motif of the magic power of the song of sailors has been inserted into a supernatural, but clearly benevolent ambience:

> Uma fragata divina   nove mezes navegou,
> Achou o mar em bonança   em Belem descarregou.
> Ella parece que é pobre   traz fazendas excellentes,
> Para ir vender a India   a partes do Oriente.
> Marinheiros que vão n'ella   levam um tão doce cantar,
> As aves dos altos ceos   nos mastros lhe vem poisar!
> Os peixinhos do mar fundo   á borda vem escutar.
> (Braga, *Açoriano,* pp. 350-51)

In other Iberian *romances,* such as the Sephardic *Chuflete* or the Catalan *Poder del canto,* there is no indication of a supernatural element, and the "magic music motif" is attached to musicians who are beyond any doubt meant to be favored by the audience.

Thus—to answer two of the initial questions—the presence of the supernatural, though without a sharp focus on the sailor, is suggested by the given combination of lyric motifs; at the same time, the sailor's song—the motif that might be expected to bear most directly on the character of the sailor—fails to identify him as an evildoer.

The preponderance of lyric elements and the suppression of the narrative may have dealt *Infante Arnaldos* the deathblow. The preference for truncated, lyric *romances* in the sixteenth century was a taste fostered by cultured poets, collectors, and editors. During the subsequent centuries, when the traditional *romances* were abandoned by the intellectuals and found refuge among the peasantry, complete stories came to be favored over the enigmatic fragments that had attracted the Spaniard of the Renaissance. Short *romances* such as *La bella en misa* were attached to narratives; even several longer stories were joined, as *Gerineldo* and *La boda estorbada* (*Condesita*). At the same time, the change of the social class that sustained the tradition, and possibly a shift in the ratio of singers from men to women, caused a loss of interest in songs of heroes or adventurous journeys and nurtured the intimate ballad of courtship, jealousy, adultery, murder, or other events that had a correlation in the experience of a village dweller. The *Romance del Infante Arnaldos* in its entirety had been forgotten on the peninsula, and the truncated version apparently neither inspired a new story that could be developed from the introduction nor was compatible with any existing narrative *romance*. A tale of abduction with an all-male cast did not fit into the modern repertoire.

El conde Olinos, on the other hand, may have been saved from extinction by its conventional situation—a young man and a girl against an implacable parent. This *romance*, sung today in Spanish-speaking communities in both the Old World and the New, has a beginning similar to that of *Infante Arnaldos*:

> Conde Niño, conde Niño, la mañana de San Juan,
> fue a dar agua a sus caballos a las orillas del mar.
> Canta unos ricos cantares que al caballo le haz parar,
> aves que van por el viento abajo les haz bajar,
> peces que están en el agua arriba les haz botar.
> (Cossío and Maza, 1:75)

A Sephardic version stresses the uncanny behavior of man and things:

> Mujeres que están en cinta de suyo habrán de abortar,
> y hombres que están por caminos y a la ciudad se volverán;
> puertas que están cerradas de suyo se abrirán;
> pájaros que están volando se paraban a escuchar.
> (Larrea, 1:183-84)

As the numerous correlations in European balladry demonstrated with regard to *Infante Arnaldos,* the motif of the effect of music on nature does not, by itself, classify the musician as man or elf, good or evil, but conforms to the neighboring motifs and the story of the ballad. In most versions of *Conde Olinos* the time and place are the same as in *Arnaldos*—the morning of Saint John's Day, on the seashore. Enhancing, and enhanced by, the extraordinary properties of the knight's song, the scene is again ready for magic or marvelous events. Even though the resemblance of the two *romances* is probably due to either unilateral or mutual contamination, the singers of both ballads must have considered the motifs appropriate for their story.[10] What, in this setting, is the nature of Olinos? What, if anything, does he have in common with the singing sailor who attracted Arnaldos? Is Olinos a not-quite-human tempter, like Ulinger or the British elf-knight, who with irresistible song lure sheltered princesses from their bowers? Is he an abductor at all? Is he a hero? Since the magic music alone does not identify him, clues must be sought in the rest of the poem for the character of Olinos as well as for the significance of his song.

The song of Olinos is heard by the queen (or countess, or in some variants, including the Portuguese, the king), who believes it is the siren's voice, and by the infanta, who knows that it is Olinos singing for her:

> Bien lo oyó la condesa   del palacio donde está.
> —Levántate, la mi hija,   si te quieres levantar,
> verás cantar la serena,   la serena de la mar.
> —La serena no sería,   la serena no será,
> que sería el conde Niño,   por mis amores lo hará.
> (Cossío and Maza, 1:75)

While the effect of the song on animate and inanimate nature is missing in a considerable number of variants, the lines about the siren accompany the song motif in every text (except a few fragmentary ones) of *Conde Olinos* and its counterparts that was available for this study—Castilian, Sephardic, Latin-American, Portuguese, and Catalan. The constancy of this motif and the dispensability of the magic effect of the song on nature suggest that the comparison of the song of Olinos with that of a siren has perhaps greater significance for this ballad.

The dialogue about the siren is found also in *romances* about prisoners condemned to die. The Portuguese Dom Pedro Pequenino is a page whose misfortune consists in having won the love of a princess. Awaiting execution, he receives in prison a visit from his mother, who asks him to play on his viol the song his father played on Saint John's Day. Dom Pedro objects at first, but then plays and sings:

> Dae vós a Deos tal mulher   tão dura do coração!
> Tem o filho para morrer,   manda tocar um baixão.

"Oh dia, que eras um dia,   oh dia de Sam João!
Quando todos os mancebos   com as suas damas vão,
Uns levam cravos e rosas,   outros um manjaricão;
Ai de mim, triste coitado   'stou n'esta escura prisão,
D'onde não vejo saír   o tão lindo claro sol.''

The simple song sounds to the king like that of an angel or a siren (the
wording used also in Portuguese versions of *Olinos*):

"Que vozes do céo são estas,   que eu aqui ouço cantar?
Ou são os anjos no céo,   ou as sereias no mar?''
"Não são os anjos no céo   nem as sereias do mar,
É Dom Pedro Pequenino,   que meu pae manda matar!''[11]

The king revokes the sentence and gives the princess to Pedro in marriage.
In a Sephardic *romance*, a young man slandered by envious courtiers and
condemned by the king saves his life in a similar manner, yielding to his
mother's request:

—Así bivas, el mi hijo,   que me cantes un cantare,
de los que cantava tu padre   noche de Pascua reale.
—¡Oh qué madre, o qué ansia,   oh qué dolor y pesare!
¡al hijo tiene en la lança,   le demanda una romança!—
Tomó santur en su mano   y empeçó su buen cantare.
El rey estava en la missa,   oyó boz de un buen cantare.
—Si ángel es de los cielos,   o sirena de la mare?
—Ni ángel es de los cielos,   ni sirena de la mare,
sino aquel mancebico   que enviatex a matare.
—Ni lo maten, ni lo toquen,   que me lo traigan delante.[12]

Ballads about a prisoner whose life is saved by his own or by a relative's
singing or playing can be found in a wide geographic range. In the German
Spielmannssohn, the young fiddler—imprisoned for the same reason as
Dom Pedro—plays at the gallows and makes the king cry. In the Danish
Harpespillet (DgF 292), Mettelille saves her brother's life by having her son
Peder play his harp. A countess, disguised as a monk, plays harp and lute
before a pagan king and receives his slave—her husband—as a reward in
the German *Graf von Rom* (*Deutsche Volkslieder,* 1:136). In the Danish
Krybskyttens Sang (DgF 384), a poacher gains his life and the king's
daughter by playing his harp. Don Francisco in the Catalan *Poder del
canto* is offered the same benefits. The brief, lyric *Gâs de Guérande* from

France tells of a score of lads who are set free when the youngest prisoner sings. But of the non-Iberian ballads only the Piedmontese *Poter del canto* mentions a siren, and in a manner quite different from the Sephardic and Portuguese *romances*: sailors stop sailing, reapers stop reaping, hoers stop hoeing, the siren stops singing.[13] The previously quoted dialogue about the siren appears to be limited to Spanish and Portuguese *romances*.

There is no indication in any of these prisoner ballads of a nonhuman origin of the musician or of supernatural intervention. The reason for the release of the prisoners is the perfection of their singing or playing; in two ballads (*Harpespillet* and *Poter del canto*) the king retains the musician in his service. It follows that the comparison to a siren or an angel will have to be interpreted as a way to describe the extreme beauty of the prisoner's song.

But besides the aesthetic, there appears to be also a moral evaluation—clearly discernible in a case where the angel-siren motif is used with no reference to singing. In the Sephardic *Buena hija,* the king, hearing a girl renounce any claim to a dowry when her father laments his poverty, exclaims: "¡Ay, válgame Dios del cielo!   ¡ay, qué bonito hablare!/¿si ángel era de los cielos   u es serena del mare?" (Bénichou, *Romancero,* p. 180).

The angel-siren motif in all these *romances* of various contents is attached to a protagonist who clearly has the balladist's sympathies and acclaim. Likewise Olinos plays in the existing texts the role of a constant lover of the princess, and victim of a cruel queen or king. In some variants, the compassionate attitude that pervades the poem is crystallized in a few lines, as in a version from Asturias that begins with "¡Quién se dol del conde Olinos,   que niño pasara el mar!" (Menéndez y Pelayo, 10:74). Olinos, in short, is a conventional hero—a hero on whose side we are told to be. The music motif enhances the hero, in approximately the same manner as winning a tournament game or wearing costly clothes highlights the heroes and heroines in other ballads.[14] The elaboration of the effect of his song on nature is one way of describing its perfection; and the comparison to the siren's song is another—with the additional effect of establishing his positive character.

What the singing of Olinos has meant to the public is demonstrated by the borrowing of the initial passage for other *romances*. In a variant of *La cautiva,* the horse is watered by the brother, the song sung by the sister, signifying her beauty. Despite the different cast, the origin of the diction is still recognizably *Conde Olinos*:

—Apártate, mora bella,   apártate, mora linda,
que va a beber mi caballo   de esas aguas cristalinas.
Mientras el caballo bebe   echó un cantar la morita.
—Vente conmigo, la dije.   —Yo contigo bien me iría.
                                    (Cossío and Maza, 1:348)

The charm of Gerineldo, sometimes shown by his silken suit and golden
shoes, is expressed in several variants through his singing, in lines obviously borrowed from *Conde Olinos*:

Una mañana de Junio   se levantó Gerineldo
a dar agua a sus caballos   a las orillas del Ebro.
Mientras los caballos beben   Gerineldo echa un cantar
y la infanta que lo oyó   le ha comenzado a llamar.[15]

Singing, clothing, and combing (or golden hair) appear alternately in the
same function in the same type of ballad, or sometimes even in different
variants of the same ballad, as in *Gerineldo,* above. Joy and happiness can
be expressed by festive clothes or by singing and playing; sorrow, by
mourning black or the silencing of music. Dom Pedro and many other
prisoners gain their freedom by their song, quite as Willie o Winsbury
(Child 100) won his life and the king's daughter with his golden hair and
pleasing attire. Silvana, who in a Sephardic text attracts her father's incestuous attention by combing her hair, in other variants plays a viol or a
guitar:

Por los jardines del Rey   paseábase Silvana un día
con la guitarra en la mano.   Oh! qué bien que la tañía!
Si bien tañe la guitarra,   mejor romance decía,
un día estando en la mesa   su padre la miraría.[16]

As a cause of unfortunate attraction, combing is particularly prevalent in
the *Romancero,* but singing is more general in the rest of Europe. In the
Piedmontese *Ratto al ballo,* a married woman's singing on the seashore
leads to seduction by the king's son and her suicide. In a Breton ballad, the
hymns sung by Saint Margaret are heard by a nobleman; her refusal to accompany him is the cause of her martyrdom. In a Danish ballad, Haagen
leads the dance on the green with a song that wakes up the queen and
draws her to the dance ground in the king's absence. The mere rumor
about Fair Else's excellent singing incites the king to abduct her. The nonhuman population, too, can be aroused by singing. A Danish watersprite

hears the song of a princess, takes the shape of her truelove, and lures her to his underwater home. In a Greek ballad, a singer barely escapes marriage to a *lamia,* but loses his flock to her. A princess in a Sephardic *romance* attracts the *culebro* by combing her hair; in the Danish *Lindormen (Dragon)*, Ingelil does the same by playing her harp.[17]

It appears from the foregoing examples that the unintentional attraction that singing or playing creates for the opposite sex, comparable to other motifs that signify beauty, is an attribute, or a passive function, different from music as a love-charm. The latter is a quasi-independent force that can be used by the good and the evil alike, as long as they know the secret of making it serve them. A great number of heroes and heroines succeed in this with the full approval of the balladist. The Danish Signelille—beguiled by the young knight and scorned by his mother—breaks the man's resistance by playing her harp and becomes his bride (DgF 265). Digenes Akrites, the hero of a Greek epic (and a ballad cycle) of this name, makes Evdokia fall in love with him by singing and playing his lute. After Soloveï Budimirovich (in a Russian *bylina*) has sung and played his harp for a whole day, Princess Zapava enters his hall and asks him to marry her.[18] Reinaldos de Montalván, who has heard that Aliarda, daughter of the Moorish king, is the most beautiful woman in the world, is received in the palace and wins her with his music:

> Don Reinaldos pidió una laúd,   que lo sabía bien tocar,
> ya comienza de tañer,   muy dulcemente a cantar,
> que todo hombre que lo oía   parecía celestial.
> Bien lo oía la infanta,   y holgaba de lo escuchar.
> (Menéndez y Pelayo, 9:121)

That Signelille, Digenes, Soloveï, and Reinaldos are positive characters is understood from the context, not from their singing. Likewise it is not the abductor's song—be he elf or human—but the pattern of subsequent events that can make him a villain. If he turns out to be the son of the king of England, as in the Catalan *Rey marinero,* he is a "good man." Ulinger and the elf-knight are evil because they try to kill the girls who have fallen under the spell of their song; so are all the sailors on whose ships the abducted girls commit suicide, and so, possibly, is Hind Etin (Child 41 A), because Lady Margaret never stops crying during her life in the wood. In *The Gypsy Laddie* (Child 200 A), the dividing line between villain and victim is curiously blurred. Johnny Faa lacks the markings of a hero, but some blame attaches also to the "fair young wanton lady," as she follows the gypsies who "sang sae sweet and sae very compleat." Here, and more clearly in the next example, the dominant actor seems to be music itself.

Like a sorcerer's apprentice, the musician sometimes releases a powerful charm and conjures forces that he cannot subdue or control. This is the case with Sir Oluf in a Danish ballad. On a bet he plays his gilded horn and draws Peder's bride Mettelille to his door. Even though he refuses to let her in, she kills herself after Peder finds out about Oluf's victory; Sir Peder mourns his lady, and Oluf avoids his presence (DgF 73). All three have become victims of their weakness; the invincible force in this ballad is love—untractable and irrevocable—represented by music. Love is a concept that does not lend itself to a description within the concrete terminology of balladry. Music, on the other hand, has a sensory image, concrete enough to conform to the diction of ballads, yet adequate in its immateriality to convey the idea of love. Also the song of Olinos has this additional nuance. Even though he is the singer and the infanta the listener—an active and a passive party—there seems to be a third force that not only compels the infanta to meet Olinos but also causes Olinos to sing, despite the imminent danger.

The theme of separated lovers, reminiscent of Hero and Leander, is discernible in a defective Sephardic version of *Conde Olinos*:

> Levantéisos vos toronja   del vuestro lindo dormir.
> Oiréis cantar hermoso   a la sirena de la mar.
> —Sirena de mar no canta   no cantó ni cantará,
> sino que es un mancebico   que me quere alcanzar.
> Si lazrará día y noche,   no me podrá alcanzar.
> Las olas de mar son muy fuertes   no las puedo navegar.
> Esto que oió el mancebo,   a la mar se fue a echar.
> —No os echéis vos, mancebo,   que esto fue mi mazal.
> (Echó su lindo trenzado   y arriba lo subió.)
> (Menéndez y Pelayo, 10:328)

This variant also gives the sea at the beginning of the more usual form of the poem a new meaning ("Conde Olinos, conde Olinos   es niño y pasó la mar," Menéndez y Pelayo, 10:72). The sea is here not the scene of abduction but the water that a man crosses to meet his love. The tone of the *romance* in all the available versions is, in fact, that of *Hero and Leander* and not of *Infante Arnaldos*; nor is it that of *Ulinger* or *Lady Isabel and the Elf-Knight*. In the songs that attract either Arnaldos or the spellbound girls, no mutuality or community is implied; but Olinos, even before his death, is shown to be as much a victim of love as the infanta ("que por mí penando está"; "que por mí llorando está").[19] The abduction ballads often make it clear that the girl has never before met the musician whose voice (or the sound of whose horn) proves irresistible; and Arnaldos shows no sign of knowing who the singing sailor is. But in many versions of *Conde Olinos* there is evidence that the princess and the count are in love before the opening scene of the *romance*. Even if we do not give a great deal of weight to Almeida Garrett's version, which states that the count had been banished by the king but came back upon the call of the princess, her disclosure that he came to marry her ("que commigo quer casar") is found also in Braga's *Romanceiro geral* (p. 37) and in many Spanish variants (where another frequent line is "que me viene a mí a buscar").

Thus the knight's song becomes a communication between separated lovers and a reactivator of their love—a function that is brought out even more clearly in the related (possibly by contamination) Catalan *Don Luis de Montalbán* (a version of *La vuelta del navegante*), where the singer is a husband who returns from the galleys and finds his wife remarried or about to remarry. As he plays his guitar, or viol, at his wife's door, the familiar dialogue about the siren ensues between the wife and the new husband and leads to the death and transformations of the original couple. A similarly communicative function of singing may be observed in Danish, Dutch, and Breton ballads.[20]

It is important to note that even when the main function of a song is communication between characters, it usually retains some of the other conventional purposes, such as indicating the beauty of the singer and acting as a love-charm on the listener. The ubiquitous ballad of the wicked mother-in-law (*La dama pastora, La gentil porquera*) gives an example of the multiple function: the young wife has been deprived of her fine dress but not of another symbol of her beauty—her lovely voice, which carries to the battlefield, or across the sea, to her husband and attracts him to the place where she is herding sheep or pigs. This motif is a standard part of the ballad in many countries, including Spain:

> —Tiene Marianita   la voz muy serena;
> me oyera don Güeso   de allá de la guerra.
> Tiene Marianita   la voz muy delgada;
> me oyera don Güeso   de allá de batalla.
> ¿Vay el caballero   por esos senderos?
> Voy a ver quién canta   en estos costeros.

¿Vay el caballero   por esos atajos?
—Voy a ver quién canta   aquí en estos altos.[21]

One might interject that all this signifies is simply the recognition of a familiar voice. But the decisive feature in the ballads in question is the limitation of this phenomenon to lovers. True to form, the queen (or king) does not recognize Olinos by his voice, but the infanta does. It follows that this function cannot be explained in realistic terms; to serve as a means of recognition and communication, the song has to be an agent of love.

The song of Olinos has thus many simultaneous functions, which not only are compatible but depend on one another: (1) The comparison of the song of Olinos to that of a siren attributes to it the greatest imaginable beauty and establishes Olinos as a positive character and as a hero; (2) the power of his song over nature supports and enhances the role of Olinos as a hero; (3) the song symbolizes his appeal to the senses (a function that in ballads is more commonly fulfilled by visual symbols of beauty); (4) with its beauty and power, the song represents another great force, too abstract for elaboration within the conventions of balladry: love; (5) as the identifying mark of the hero and as the poetic equivalent of love, the song is a means of recognition and of communication between lovers.

The song of Olinos offers no evidence of being anything but the song of a lover. No element of abduction is discernible; the villain of the story is the infanta's mother (or father), who causes the death of the lovers. With so strong an emphasis on his positive character, Olinos is unlikely to hail from supernatural antecedents, since such elvish seducers as Halewijn are known to have lost in the course of transmission their nonhuman but not their villainous characteristics. Yet, there is in *Conde Olinos* a series of suggestive introductory motifs similar to those in *Infante Arnaldos,* though in a somewhat lesser concentration—Saint John's Day, the seashore, sporadically also the magic effect of the song on man and nature—which seem to announce supernatural happenings.

A supernatural theme indeed becomes prominent in the second half of *Conde Olinos*: after their untimely death, Olinos and the infanta reappear as plants, birds, and in many variants as a shrine, altar image, or healing spring, as discussed in chapter 7. These transformations on the one hand confirm that Olinos cannot be anything but a hero or anything but human, since otherwise an intervention of higher justice on his behalf would seem highly irregular. On the other hand, the transformations justify the composition of the introductory passage: while the suggestion of the supernatural has apparently no reference to the hero's identity, it does create a propitious atmosphere for the marvelous transformations.

Allowing for all the variety in the character of the musicians and in the development of the stories, the music in the ballads discussed up to now can be said to express an ideal concept—supreme beauty or supreme love, or a fusion of both. There is, however, another application of the music motif that lacks such totality, an application that could be called picaresque: love is reduced to liaison, irresistible beauty to calculated inveigling. What follows is a series of examples that will clarify the difference and might ultimately assist in defining the basic objectives in the use of the music motif.

In *La esposa de don García,* music (as in other variants of the ballad festive clothing) implies an unsavory relationship between the abducted lady and her Moorish captors. Don García's mother, who wants him to believe that his wife was a willing captive of the Moors, says she was dressed in red and played a viol: "Vihuela de oro en sus manos   y muy bien que la tangía./Cada vuelta que le daba,   cuernos, cuernos, don García." The foregoing slander is contradicted by the wife's aunt, or mother: "Vihuela de oro en las manos,   de pesar no la tangía."[22] Belonging to the same category, in Sephardic, Canarian, and Portuguese *romances*, is the serenade of a man at the door of a married woman as a manifestation of an illicit relationship:

> Yo me alevantí un lunes   y un lunes por la mañana,
> tomí mi arco en mi mano   y ordení esta cántica,
> ¿ánde la fuera a tañer?   a puertas de mi namorada.

The woman answers that she cannot open the door, since "al hijo tengo en el pecho   y al marido en la cama" (Bénichou, *Romancero,* p. 142).

A singing prisoner may be a sincere young man whose angelic voice saves him from undeserved death and makes him the son-in-law of a king, or he may be a scheming scoundrel such as the Moor in *El moro cautivo y la infanta*:

> Estábase el morito   en las cárceles muy hondas;
> cantando iba el cantar nuevo   de todos sus animales,
> un cantar que canta el moro   un cantar y atán hermoso.

> Por ahí pasara la infanta   que de él se enamorare.
> —Por tu vida, y el morito,   cautivo del rey mi padre,
> que cantes el cantar nuevo   que has cantado el primer galle.
> —De cantar la mi señora,   de buen gusto cantaría;
> las cárceles son muy hondas,   la voz no me alcanzaría.[23]

The princess steals the keys to the jail and rides away with the fugitive, who, at a safe distance, reveals that he is married, whereupon the princess "muerta cae en un desmayo."

One of the less usual practical applications of music is making the adversary dance. The Danish Dame Gundelil is approached in her husband's absence by the king, who promises her vast domains if she will play her harp. She saves her honor and gains all the wealth, as her playing compels the king, his men, and his horse to dance (DgF 236). In a Bulgarian ballad Memed, whose tambourine makes him irresistible to all women, is brought before a court, where he makes the judge, the bishop, and the other dignitaries dance; when the judge finds that the power lies in the tambourine, Memed is set free (*Deutsche Volkslieder,* 3:173). While no actual blame attaches to Memed, and Gundelil is clearly virtuous, the bizarre visual image of compulsive dancing precludes an idealized impression of the music motif.

Another ambiguous quality is the soporific effect of music. On the one hand it is the test of the perfect musician, appearing as such in the case of Glenkindie, "the best harper/That ever harped on a string" (Child 67 B), whose mastery of the art is illustrated by the effect his music has on nature, and who harps everybody in the king's court, except the young countess, to sleep:[24]

> He's taen his harp intill his hand,
> He's harpit them a' asleep,
> Except it was the young countess,
> That love did waukin keep.

But the feat of Glenkindie—a noble lover—is duplicated by his man Gib, "a wild loon," who plays his master to sleep and visits the lady in his stead.

Despite his evil character, the elf-knight, who in Child 4 B also harps the king and his court to sleep, cannot be classified with Glenkindie's man Gib. Gib is a cad; the elf-knight and his counterparts Halewijn and Ulinger, before the later versions turned them into plain criminals (and omitted the song motif), were sinister characters of a certain magnitude, endowed with a primitive power rather than picaresque cunning. The dividing line is often vague; the same theme can be cast in a lyrical or a sportive form. The sailor who sings the abducted girl to sleep in the Catalan *Rey marinero* is neither a villain nor a prankster but a fairy-tale prince carrying off his bride; the soporific song is a part of the fabulous adventure: "Amb el cant del mariné s' ha 'dormideta,/y amb els ayres de la mar ella 's desperta" (Milá, p. 151). It is interesting to note that in the Sephardic version of *Infante Arnaldos,* on which Menéndez Pidal bases his reconstruction ("Poesía popular," p. 65), the count falls asleep, not from the sailor's song but the sound of water: "Alzan velas, caen remos, comienzan a navegar;/con el ruïdo del agua el sueño le venció ya." It may be puzzling that the song, powerful enough to draw the count aboard, does not also put him to sleep, as it does in another Sephardic variant: "—Quien mi cantar quiere oír, a mi galera ha de entrar./Al són de los dulces cantos, el conde dormido se ha" (Bénichou, *Romancero,* p. 207). However, *Infante Arnaldos* conforms in this respect to a stylistic convention. Even though one symbol can do multiple duties, there seems to be a reluctance to overwork the same symbol within a given ballad: where the sailor's song is the lure, it usually does not reappear in the text as a soporific. The latter function is, on the other hand, a standard feature in the variants of *Rey marinero,* where the girl boards the ship to get silk for her embroidery. In the variant of *Infante Arnaldos,* quoted above, where the song doubles as a soporific, both functions are drawn together into the same passage, so that a repetition is avoided. Thus it is unlikely that these ballads deal with two different kinds of singing; the power of song has numerous manifestations, and the balladist chooses now one, now another.

In the Russian *Tzar Solomon and Solomonida,* the creators of the *bylina* have succeeded in preserving the charm of music by separating it— by a hairsbreadth as it may be—from the device that actually accomplishes an unethical project. The outfitting of the three scarlet ships, on which Tzar Solomon's wife is to be abducted, is presented in an orientally sensuous form, with the music motif serving more as an ornament than a device: "Set a tree of cypress, and on it place birds of paradise that they may sing imperial songs. Prepare a couch of ivory, and at its head place . . . a little gusly, which will sing, hum, breathe forth delicate tones of itself—all the airs of Tzargrad." Then, however, the schemer Tarakashko adds a practical hint: "Roll on board noble vodka, and the drink that bringeth oblivion of all things." After Tarakashko has succeeded in making the Tzaritza drunk, the *gusly* (dulcimer or psalterion) emits the soporific tones without the sullying touch of the knave: "The Tzaritza lay down upon the fair couch, the little harp sounded softly, the birds of heaven sang, and the Tzaritza fell asleep."[25]

On the other hand, music can be the axis of a picaresque theme even when the musician and his action are perfectly condonable. In a Danish ballad Verner, brought from the dungeon to entertain the chatelaine and her ladies, does not gain his freedom by moving their hearts with the beauty of his song, but sings them asleep and steals the keys from the wall (DgF 383). By the same means the young man trapped by the wild woman of the mountain saves his life in numerous variants of *La Serrana* from the Canary Islands:

> Acabando de cenar,   vigüela de oro me entrega.
> Y yo como lo sabía hacer,   me puse a templar la cuerda;
> con el son de la vigüela   la serrana se durmiera.
> *(La flor de la marañuela,* 1:177)

The Sea Captain, from Newfoundland, reverses the usual application of music in abduction ballads; the girl who has been lured on board begins to sing: "She sang so neat, so sweet and complete,/She sang sailors and captain to sleep." She robs the sailors of silver, gold, and other costly ware, and paddles to the shore with the captain's broadsword; from dry land she mocks the captain that she is "a maiden once more on the shore."[26]

The blind Lochmaben Harper (Child 192A) even steals King Henry's horse with the approval of the ballad audience:

> And ay he harpit, and ay he carpit,
>   Till a' the lords had fitted the floor;
> They thought the music was sae sweet,
>   And they forgot the stable-door.
>
> And ay he harpit, and ay he carpit,
>   Till a' the nobles were sound asleep;
> Then quietly he took aff his shoon,
>   And safly down the stair did creep.

But when a theft is committed on a mythical scale, for the benefit of a nation, it loses any picaresque connotation. Väinämöinen's song in the *Kalevala* (Poem 42), which lulls the people of Pohjola to sleep and enables

the singer to carry away the Sampo (the mill of plenty), is an act of hero-
ism and not of mischief. His ability to sing man and nature-spirits asleep is
a part of the superhuman stature of the primeval Finnish musician.

On the whole the ignoble roles of music can be found more frequently in
newer ballads, while the eulogistic elaborations belong largely to earlier
stock. In part this difference is due to a noticeable shift in popular balladry in general—from heroic and idealistic to picaresque and prurient. But
there may be another reason also, which has to do with the singers' moti-
vation from a professional standpoint.

When a minstrel sang about singing, he had a vested interest in his song;
by shedding favorable light on music, he could make propaganda for himself and his art. A northern Russian *bylina* that tells a story of musicians
whose playing works miracles—punishes detractors, rewards supporters,
and conquers a pagan czar—may have been, as Trautmann (pp. 375-78)
believes, the creation of a clever singer who wanted to vindicate the honor
and dignity of his profession during the harassment in the seventeenth century. An earlier *bylina* of the Kiev cycle hints that the small space on the
earthen oven assigned to the minstrel in Prince Vladimir's banquet hall is
not worthy of a singer of heroic deeds (Hapgood, p. 203).

The influence of the court minstrel is illustrated, or perhaps wishfully
described, in the Scottish ballad *Hind Etin* (Child 41 A) by the distribution
of the three royal rings that Lady Margaret gives her eldest son by which to
gain entrance into the king's palace:

> "Ye'll gie the first to the proud porter,
>   And he will lat you in;
> Ye'll gie the next to the butler-boy,
>   And he will show you ben;
>
> "Ye'll gie the third to the minstrel
>   That plays before the king;
> He'll play success to the bonny boy
>   Came thro the wood him lane."

In order to achieve and maintain admiration and awe for his profession
among the audience, the singer reached for hyperbole and fantasy in order
to enhance those qualities of music that were known empirically. Music as
a sleep-inducer is an everyday experience; that the young man in *La
Serrana* is able to play the mountain woman asleep after a heavy meal does

not exceed the dimensions of such experience. But many ballads expand this quality: not just one tired huntress, but a palaceful of courtiers falls asleep. Similarly within reality is the attraction that a musician exerts on the listener. The use of the guitar by the man in *La adúltera* to make a woman amenable is a reflection of reality without imaginative reworking. But again, most ballads amplify the effect: princesses fall in love with the musician, chaste maidens follow him on land and sea. Likewise the remuneration that a good musician would be likely to receive grows into such fabulous benefits as a last-minute pardon from the gallows and the status of son-in-law to the king.

From hyperbole, the threshold to fantasy is easy to cross. That the wayfarer turns back or that the reaper stops in his work to hear an excellent singer is still within human experience—at least within imaginable human experience—but almost imperceptibly the effect extends into the unreal: birds stop to listen, fish come to the surface, water springs from a stone, doors open by themselves, and the forces of the otherworld yield their victims.

As we could observe earlier, neither the moral character nor the classification of the musician as human or nonhuman can be determined by his ability to practice the art or by its power over men, animals, and things. There are, further, no separate kinds of music such as "evil" music and "good" music, love music and sleep music. All music has a multifarious but constant power that is manifested according to the context of each ballad. What the minstrel appears to want most is to create the impression that music has superb power—if need be, superb sinister power—which makes the musician a person to be both revered and feared.

Sometimes there remains no doubt that a singer has expanded and embroidered the motif of the magic effect of song with no other purpose than that of extolling music and musicians. The most imaginative and exuberant expression can be found in the Finnish *Kalevala,* where it is usually Väinämöinen who sings and plays his harp so that mountains echo, boulders crash, crags shake, rocks splash into the billows, and gravel boils in the water. Also the spirits that inhabit nature are affected by Väinämöinen's harp: Tapio, master of the Woodland, and his wife listen; the Virgins of the Air listen from the rainbow and clouds; the Moon Spirit and the Sun Spirit spoil their weaving; Ahto, king of the waves, comes to the surface. The Spirits of Goldeneye drop their golden and silver brushes; the mistress of the water falls asleep. When Väinämöinen plays at home, the roof echoes, the floors thud, the ceiling sings, the doors roar, the windows rejoice, the stove stones stir (Poems 41, 44). Poor singing, however, is not only ludicrous but causes calamity. Thus, Lemminkäinen "began to intone, began poor man, to sing/with his harsh voice, with his raspy throat . . ./the mouth moved, the beard shook, the jaws were askew." A crane heard the singing and, frightened by the bad voice, started "shrieking crossly, screaming angrily./With that it wakened North Farm, aroused the evil domain," and sparked off a series of disasters (Poem 42).

A similar distinction between a masterful musician and bunglers is expounded in the Sephardic *El chuflete,* which, in the opinion of Menéndez Pidal, was known in Spain at the time when *Infante Arnaldos* acquired the magic-song motif. The *chuflete,* a pipe that nobody has been able to play, is finally blown by the right person, with miraculous effects on woman, child, and ship:

> La parida que está pariendo   sin dolor la hizo parir,
> la criatura que está llorando   sin tetar la hizo dormir,
> la nave que está en el golfo   al porto la hizo salir.[27]

Armistead and Silverman conclude their discussion of *El chuflete* with a summary of the numerous applications of magic music in European balladry:

In most of the above-cited ballads, the magic music serves some clearly defined purpose: Count Olinos sings a courting song; *La canción del huérfano* and *Il poter del canto* win the singers their freedom; the Greek songs are lamentations; the British and Scandinavian examples wake the dead, inspire affection, effect a rescue from an otherworldly being, or place mortals under elfin power. Everywhere such miraculous effects are merely ancillary to the music's major purpose. In *El chuflete,* on the other hand, the magic flute's *raison d'être* in itself constitutes one of the ballad's mysteries. Apparently the flute sounds forth and works its joyous miracles upon the ambient world just for the sheer marvel of it and that is, perhaps, the very best purpose of all. (*Judeo-Spanish Ballad Chapbooks,* p. 365)

It certainly was "the very best purpose of all" from the standpoint of those who made and sang not only this *romance,* but also many others. The identity of the author, rather than that of the fictional musician within the ballad, will allow us to find consistency among the innumerable folk songs that use the motif in question. Earlier in this chapter, the analysis of *Infante Arnaldos* and *Conde Olinos* reached the conclusion that the magic-music motif could not be accepted as evidence of the supernatural character of either of the two singers. Nor did their singing establish a kinship with the sinister seducers, Halewijn, Ulinger, and the elf-knight. The song of Olinos, quite to the contrary, was found to enhance his role as a positive hero; the short version of *Infante Arnaldos* must be considered noncommittal as to the nature and the purposes of the sailor.

Thus, as long as the moral stature of the singer or the plot of the ballad is taken as the main criterion, the large variety of situations and the assortment of heroes and villains may create the impression that the magic-music motif has been used by balladists in an erratic or even meaningless manner. Only when the magic song or music is seen as a separate entity—reflecting more directly upon the creator and performer of the ballad than upon its fictional hero—can the existence of the motif in so many different contexts be satisfactorily explained.

If we now look again at the truncated version of *Infante Arnaldos,* its affinity to the ballads that focus upon song itself, as *El chuflete,* stands out clearly. The introductory motifs with their hints at a supernatural imminence and the suspense created by the invitation, with which the best-known version ends, appear subservient to the glorification of music. While in many other ballads a music motif supports the action as much as the action provides an opportunity to display the power of music, the balladist here has discarded the balance in "mutual assistance" and has made his own art the central theme.

But the larger-than-life image of the singer has become scarce. *El chuflete,* as well as *Infante Arnaldos,* has disappeared from the peninsula; in many variants of *Conde Olinos* the passages that elaborate the power of song have dwindled to perfunctory mention; *romances* that appear to be of recent origin seldom make much of music or musicians. The texts in the living tradition place guitar and viol in the hands of the crafty and the wanton. It may well be that with the demise of professional minstrels the idealization of music lost its main promoters.

7

METEMPSYCHOSIS OR MIRACLE

Transformations in *Conde Olinos*

While Count Olinos emerged from the previous chapter as human, regardless of the magic effect of his song, the last portion of the *romance* undeniably deals with supernatural events. A deludingly handy explanation of these events is usually given: namely, that the final portion of the ballad is a poetic exposition of transmigration of souls. The erudite exercise of tracing the transformation motif back to the pre-Christian belief in metempsychosis is a rather easy one, but it is just an erudite exercise and not necessarily indicative of what is seen in this ballad by the singers and their audience. To rely exclusively on the earliest strains of thought and belief that may have inspired the creators of the initial forms of a motif is to take the position that an idea as fixed in a ballad is immune to the passage of time and that the countless changes in diction that occur in the course of transmission are nothing but variations on an immutable theme. I believe we should ask more often whether the changes in details are not symptomatic of changes in the philosophy of the ballad.

I propose to examine the transformation motif in *Conde Olinos* as it is sung today. The appeal of the ballad is undoubtedly still strong, since it is thriving in many parts of Spain and the rest of the Hispanic world, but the appeal of each version need not derive from the same ideas. Let us assess the motif and decide whether the reasons for the popularity of *Conde Olinos* are as atavistic as a scholar of primitive religions might surmise.

As a concomitant of the idea of metempsychosis, it is usually taken for granted that the main effort of the migrating souls in *Conde Olinos* is to prove that love endures beyond death. Appealing as this interpretation may be, it fails to take into account a frequent version in which any such message has been all but deleted. A reevaluation should, therefore, also help determine how love has been faring as the ruling sentiment.

Most versions of *Conde Olinos* begin on the morning of Saint John's Day, as Olinos sings a marvelous song while watering his horse.[1] The queen believes she hears a siren's voice, but then the princess speaks up: it is Count Olinos, and the song is for her. The mother has the noble singer killed, and the girl dies shortly thereafter, either from heartbreak, from choice, or upon the queen's orders. Here begins the motif of transformations. From the two graves spring plants—olive, lemon, orange, grapefruit, or pear trees, or a rose and a briar, whose branches embrace:

> De él salió un bello olivo,   de ella salió un naranjar:
> como se querían tanto,   rama con rama se dan.
> (Schindler, texts, p. 55)

The similarity to the British rose-briar commonplace (*Lord Thomas and Fair Annet, Lord Lovel,* etc.) is obvious. The British songs have several different stories, but the ending is uniform: from the graves of two lovers grows a rose-briar or birch-briar pair, and the branches intertwine in a lover's knot. Tragic love ballads close with affectionate grave-plants also in many other European areas: Germany, the Piedmont, Yugoslavia, Albania, Greece, Hungary. The source most often suggested for this motif is the medieval story of *Tristan and Isolt,* but there are also classical antecedents, such as the tale of Philemon and Baucis. The motif has been found to exist outside Europe and even outside Indo-Germanic boundaries, in Egypt, Afghanistan, China, and Japan.

Compared with similar lines in some other languages, certain versions of *Conde Olinos* display perhaps a more impressive number of features that emphasize the immortality of love and, at the same time, can be related to a belief in metempsychosis. As in the text quoted above, there is usually a statement that each plant originated in one of the dead lovers, or even that the lovers became plants: "del uno nació," "salió," or "ella se volvió un olivo." The plants embrace, kiss, and weep. When the queen decrees their destruction, they either grow again or return in a new form. In several English ballads the rose and briar are cut down, but here the destruction appears to be irreversible and the destroyer is a *deus ex machina* (the clerk or the priest of the parish, an old woman, a cold northeasterly or northwesterly wind), not an antagonist previously known to the audience, as in *Conde Olinos.*[2]

Besides illustrating the passage of souls into plants and the kind of love that outlasts death, the details enumerated above bring *Conde Olinos* close to the tale of *Tristan and Isolt*; closer, indeed, than the motif found in other countries, where the destruction is either totally missing, or unjustified and not followed by regrowth.

A peculiarly Spanish development is the rebirth of the lovers as birds, after being cut down as plants. In some variants, the birds emerge from the milk and the royal blood that spurt from each plant respectively during the destruction:

> Del uno salía leche,   del otro sangre real;
> de la leche una paloma,   de la sangre un gavilán.
>   (Cossío and Maza, no. 35)[3]

The most usual combinations are dove and hawk, as above, or two doves. In the versions where the transformation into birds concludes the series, they often fly together into the sky (though the word *cielo* stands for both sky and heaven—an ambiguity that will be of interest later in the discussion of the dove).

Multiple transformations are extremely rare in European balladry. Even La Villemarqué's version of the Breton *Aotrou Nann,* often used as an example of two-stage transmigration, makes no statement to the effect that the two oaks that arise from the common tomb, or the two white doves that sing on the branches and fly at dawn toward the skies, are the count and his wife; nor is there any destruction of the oaks.[4] In contrast, the transformations in *Conde Olinos* are not only clearly identified but even reiterated in the third stage, which will presently be discussed: the princess (or, exceptionally, Olinos) recalls "when we were olive trees," or "when we were doves"—unequivocal statements that are matched perhaps only in eastern European ballads (Hungarian, Lithuanian, Russian).

Thus the versions of *Conde Olinos* that end with the regrowth of the plants after destruction, or their rebirth as birds, appear to preserve the ideas of metempsychosis and undying love with extraordinary clarity. However, as will be shown below, some of the very elements that seem to reinforce the foregoing ideas contribute actually to their deterioration. Both the repeated intervention of a logical antagonist and the prolonged series of transformations have led to a radical altering of the philosophical axis.

The version that is favored in northern Spain but crops up also in many other parts of the Peninsula and in North Africa does not stop at the bird phase but develops the transformations further. The queen commands that the birds be shot, but they turn into a shrine—usually a chapel and an altar, which may be accompanied by a spring. The shrine has healing powers of which the queen has need, but she is rebuffed by the voice in the shrine:

> —Quítese de ahí, mala reina,   de ahí se puede quitar,
> cuando éramos olivos   bien nos mandaba cortar,
> cuando éramos palomas   bien nos mandaba tirar,
> y ahora que somos ángeles   no te queremos curar.
> (Cossío and Maza, no. 35)

There is a version from Asturias that I would consider the connecting step between the shrine version and those previously discussed: the destroyed olive trees reappear as a spring and a river, where those who suffer from lovesickness go to bathe:

> D' ella naciera una fuente,   d' él nació un río caudal.
> "Quien tuviere mal de amores   aquí se venga a bañar."
> La Reina que aquello oyera   también se fuera a lavar.
> —Detente, Reina, detente,   no me vengas dexobar.
> Cuando yo era Blanca Flor   tú me mandaste matar;
> cuando yo era verde oliva   tú me mandaste cortar;
> ahora soy fuente clara,   non me puedes facer mal;
> para todos he de correr   para ti me he de secar.
> (Menéndez y Pelayo, 10:74-75)

Here the retribution is in keeping with the crime, considering that love was what the queen persecuted and *mal de amores* is what the healing waters refuse to cure. However, in the versions where the healing properties belong to a shrine, the queen has physical ailments. Frequently she has lost the sight in one eye, and the shrine counters her request for a cure with a pronouncement that her other eye will become blind also:

> —Si eres tuerta de un ojo,   de los dos te has de quedar,
> dos amantes se querían   y los mandasteis matar.
> (Catalán, p. 219)

In other variants, the spring declares that the queen shall die within three days, or she enters the chapel and is crushed by a falling cornice.

It should be added that in Portuguese versions from the Azores the shrine lacks both the power to heal and the vindictive attitude. When the king, who is the persecutor, goes to the chapel, his daughter tells him to wipe away his tears and impresses upon him that parents must not set asunder marriages made by God (Braga, *Açoriano,* pp. 272-75).

The thriving of the phase with the miraculous shrine is the principal manifestation of a tendency to shift the entire motif away from metempsychosis toward a Christian context. Chapel and altar obviously belong to the latter. The spring is a more flexible entity: the spring and stream that cure lovesickness in a version of *Conde Olinos* have no recognizable Christian sanction, and fairy springs are known in pre-Christian mythology; however, the pagan associations have been largely superseded by miraculous springs in shrines of the Virgin Mary. Also the place where a martyr has died is wont to be marked by a spring, as in the *romance* of *Delgadina,* who died because she rejected her father's incestuous approaches (Cossío and Maza, 1:300, 301, 303, 306, 309). Indeed, martyrdom and consequent sainthood appear to be the underlying concept in the shrine version of *Conde Olinos.* When the daughter's voice speaks in the shrine, she identifies herself and Olinos as angels or as saints, who died by the hand of the queen. The reasoning is similar to that of the *romance* of *Ilenia* (Menéndez y Pelayo, 10:211): about to enter a convent, Ilenia is abducted and killed by an insistent suitor; she becomes a chapel, which announces to the supplicant murderer that neither she nor the King of Heaven will grant him pardon. In the rationale of *Conde Olinos* it seems to be immaterial that the young couple died for love, and not for religious faith or Christian virtue.

That the miracle-revenge phase has become the principal one in the successive transformations is shown by several contractions in the rest of the motif. Some stages, most often the birds, are likely to be omitted; the lovers may be changed immediately into a chapel and an altar; or the healing properties are assigned to a tree or a spring that appears between the graves, without any intermediate transformations. In one variant, the altar is built from the wood of the grave-tree upon the queen's orders.

As the miraculous shrine gains importance, the details associated with metempsychosis show a marked decline. In many cases the embrace of the grave-plants is lacking, as is the flow of milk and blood from the felled trees (in a Sephardic version from Morocco the milk and royal blood issue from the corpses before their transformation into plants). The last change is particularly indicative of the shift in the framework, since bleeding trees are a familiar feature in the motif of metempsychosis: when a tree inhabited by a soul is cut, it is likely to bleed and to speak in its own defense (Balys, p. 113; Leader, p. 183).

Both the appeal of the shrine version and the irrelevance of metempsychosis can be observed even in Sephardic texts from Morocco. Thus an explicit mention of transformation may be avoided, but the healing powers retained:

> Entre una tierra y otra   prezide un limonar
> con una hierba muy santa   que muchos ciegos curará.
>
> (Larrea, 1:180)

As in the peninsular shrine version, the focus is on the punishment of the queen—double blindness—though without a direct identification of the implacable daughter with the grave-plants.

Some shorter versions also show a suppression of metempsychotic elements; at the same time,the singers have been reluctant to discard the lyric aspect of the plants and birds. In a Sephardic version from the Levant that concludes abruptly with the execution of the lovers, the introductory verses faintly echo the plant and bird stages of the transmigration:

> En el vergel de la reina   cresía un buen rosal,
> en la ramica más alta   un rusción sentí cantar.
>
> (Menéndez y Pelayo, 10:307)

A Sephardic compromise is found also in *El pájaro verde*—a *romance* of analogous content, to which the ending of *Conde Olinos* is sometimes grafted:

> Entierran a los dos juntos   juntitos en una caja
> él parecía un clavel,   ella una rosa temprana.
>
> (Larrea, 1:226)

Similarly, the Venezuelan *Corrido de los pajarillos*—otherwise clearly recognizable as a version of *Conde Olinos*—reduces the number of transformations to zero and retains only some separate elements of the motif. The daughter, asking to die with her lover, requests that he be buried in the church and she under the altar, on her breast a dove and on his a hawk: "En mi pecho una paloma,   en su pecho un gavilán."[5] One cannot attribute this mutation of the motif to a possible total rejection of the irrational, since the ballad has received, in exchange as it were, the addition of an introductory section about the miraculous power of the unicorn. What is rejected is the idea of metempsychosis. Nor can one speak in this version of love triumphant, since the dove and the hawk have lost their meaning of resurrected lovers. Love is still powerful, but only as an absolute that permits no compromise, and for which the only alternative is death.

In other instances, both in the shrine version and in the shorter ones, the originally supernatural occurrences are given rational explanations. Thus, when the plants grow anew after destruction, the reason is the viability of their trunks: "Como el tronco era verde, siempre volvió a rebrotar" (Catalán, p. 209; cf. p. 211; Cossío and Maza, no. 41). Similarly, the reason the birds cannot be killed is that they are flying or that the sharpshooter is too young: "como eran aves volantes, no las pudieron matar" (Schindler, texts, p. 54); "el tirador era niño, nunca los pudo acertar" (Cossío and Maza, no. 36). One cannot help but suspect a weakening of the singers' faith in the power of love as they resort to positivistic reasoning.

In the shrine version the plants often are destroyed because of the nuisance they create: they do not let the queen pass, or they tear her apron or skirt on her way to Mass. The birds eat the queen's cherries, peck her plate, or sit on the king's shoulder and table.[6] It may be that the identity of the plants and birds is not evident to the antagonist, so that their destruction without a new offense on their part would seem illogical. In any case these rather innocuous verses have a startling effect on the ideological direction: the main business of the transformed couple is plainly to harass the enemy rather than to perpetuate their love, all the more as in the Spanish version the lines about the annoyance replace those that described the embrace of the plants.

That the bird phase—the most expendable in the shrine version—has survived at all, is probably due to connotations other than metempsychosis.

Paloma and *gavilán* (dove and sparrow-hawk, one of the usual pairings in *Conde Olinos*), particularly in this combination, but also singly, are popular terms for "sweethearts." Dove and hawk have this function in songs of Spain and Latin America; also the gaucho Martín Fierro, in the epic poem by that name, tells how during his absence his woman had flown away with a "hawk." Hence, the connotation of "lovers" undoubtedly adheres to the *paloma-gavilán* pair in *Conde Olinos*.[7]

Even here, however, religious symbolism is likely to have at least equal weight. The bird that appears most frequently in the transformation motif is the dove, either together with a hawk or as a pair (thus also in several variants of the Catalan *Don Luis de Montalbán*). Even though the primitive concept of the soul-bird looms in the background, a more recent influence on *Conde Olinos* must be sought in the dove as a Christian symbol, not only in the Scriptures, but also in the visual arts and balladry itself. The dove symbolizes the soul in Visigothic and Romanesque art; in religious painting of even later date, the dove represents the Holy Ghost, as it does in the account of the baptism of Christ, Matthew 3:16. Braga (*Romanceiro geral,* p. 184) points out that in the Latin hymn of Saint Eulalia the soul of the righteous ascends to heaven as a dove. In European balladry, likewise, a dove often signifies the soul of an innocent person. In Danish ballads (and similarly in German ones), doves escort the soul, which becomes one of them, to heaven, while ravens take the guilty soul to hell. Breton ballads and tales often show a crow and a white dove battling for a soul; also a saved soul or the Holy Ghost can appear as a dove. In the Spanish *romance* of *Delgadina* (Cossío and Maza, 1:301), the deathbed of the martyred girl is surrounded by angels, with a dove—the Holy Virgin—in the middle. Another Spanish song shows three doves in a liturgical setting:

> Tres palomitas
> en un palomar
> suben y bajan
> al pie del altar;
> tocan a misa,
> alaban a Dios,
> Santa María,
> ruega por nos.
> (Cossío and Maza, 2:313)

Thus the image of doves in *Conde Olinos* lends the lovers an aura of purity, righteousness, or even sanctity. The suggestion of saved souls is further enhanced by the dual meaning of *cielo* (sky, heaven), to which the birds ascend in the versions that conclude with this phase.[8] These associations may also be a reason for the failure of the queen's sharpshooters to hit the birds, which occurs more frequently than a failure to fell the trees. In Cossío and Maza, no. 35, the unscathed birds fly to the seashore, where they establish a shrine and proceed to heal the sick; in the dialogue with the queen they identify themselves as angels. Evidently the transformation from birds to chapel and altar was felt to be superfluous, since the birds in themselves represented the sublime stage of the human soul.

The point that I should like to make here is this: perhaps it is inaccurate to assume that the associations of the bird phase changed after it had become established in the tradition. Possibly the birds, from the start, were meant to be souls in visible form, on their way to heaven, rather than bodies inhabited by the souls of lovers.

The shrine version differs from the shorter ones in two somewhat incompatible aspects: the terminology is Christian (angels, saints, image of Virgin, chapel, altar) and so is the reasoning that martyrdom leads to sainthood, but the two creatures who profess to be saints or angels are imbued with a spirit of eye-for-eye justice. This is in contrast to the gentle attitude of the more overtly pagan forms, which celebrate the victory of love with a resurrection of the plants or a flight of the birds into infinity, leaving the queen with her physical persecution in the low realm of matter, unworthy of further attention. But when the lovers in the shrine version get even with their adversary, they seem to operate on the queen's own level.[9]

This kind of even contest with a tangible victory brings *Conde Olinos* close to the two types of popular tales that Child (1:401) mentions as probable sources and influences in his discussion of *The Twa Magicians*: (1) A youth and a maid transform themselves by the magical power of one or the other into various shapes that enable them to elude, and finally to escape, the pursuing sorcerer, fiend, giant, or ogre; (2) the sorcerer's apprentice and his master, who is pursuing him, assume various shapes, until the fugitive manages to take on the stronger figure and dispatches his adversary. On closer scrutiny, *Conde Olinos* contains more features of these two types of tales than does *The Twa Magicians*. The similarity between the Spanish ballad and the first category of tales lies not only in the numerical relation (one pursuing two), but also in the dissimilar means of combat: the fugitives go through a series of defensive transformations, while the aggressor does not necessarily change his shape, but wields his power in some other way. The second type of tale coincides with the Spanish poem in the turning of tables at the end of the story: the underdog acquires superiority and hits back.

The resemblance to fairy tales is further heightened in several variants of the shrine version by the omission of the destruction of the plants and birds, or by the failure of attempted destruction, before their emergence in a new form:

Ella se volvío paloma　y él se volvió palomar
y al palacio de la reina　se fueron a aposentar.
La reina que les ha visto　les ha mandado tirar,
y el tirador que les tira　no les ha llegado a dar.
Desde allí tomaron vuelo　a las orillas del mar;
ella se volvió una ermita　y él se volvió un rico altar.
(Cossío and Maza, no. 45)

When the queen goes to cure her eyes, the voice reminds her that she had given orders to kill her daughter, then to cut her down as an olive tree and to shoot her as a dove, but that now she cannot tear her down as a chapel—a proclamation of victory. Thus the transformations create an impression of a contest by shapeshifting, as it occurs in the fairy tales mentioned above and in many others.[10] Even the wording, "se volvió," suggests shapeshifting rather than transmigration of souls. In the variants where the plants and birds create a petty nuisance to the inimical parent, the contest becomes almost humorous:[11]

De ella salió una paloma,　de él un rico palomar.
Cuando la reina cenaba,　el plato iban a pipiar.
La reina cuando lo ha visto　los ha mandado cazar.
(Cossío and Maza, no. 37)

Familiar from fairy tales also is the type of justice exercised in the final outcome of *Conde Olinos*: not only does the initial victim rise and crush the villain, but the punishment is conventionally ruthless. Wicked stepmothers in Spanish tales are thrown into boiling oil; the final fate of the queen in the *romance* is death or total blindness.

Perhaps such similarities to fairy tales have enhanced the appeal of *Conde Olinos* to children—several existing versions are girls' play-songs—which, in turn, may have brought about other changes. When the daughter's voice speaks in the shrine, she accuses the queen of having killed her "cuando yo era pequeñita" or "chiquitita." Inconsistent as it seems at first glance, the adoption of the ballad by children may have caused, in turn, an intentional braking of the trend toward fairytale-like cruelty. The variants collected as play-songs, where the princess's first-person pronouncement of merciless vengeance on the queen may have been vetoed by the mothers of the little girls who sang the ballad, show a relatively mellow ending:

Cuando yo era chiquitita   tú me mandaste matar,
y ahora que soy fuentecita   agua no te quiero dar.
(*Cancionero popular de Madrid,* 1:93)

Likewise the reduction of the queen's ailment to a sore finger (Cossío and Maza, nos. 41-44), as well as the backhanded pardon that the shrine grants in some variants ("pero por ser la mi madre,   unas gotas te he de dar," and other similar lines, Cossío and Maza, nos. 36, 40, 45) may be conscious alterings for the benefit of children.

If the versions of *Conde Olinos* are grouped by the underlying concepts, the plant and plant-bird versions will be found to express the enduring quality of love, while all the versions that culminate in the denial of a cure to the queen satisfy primarily the sense of justice. The metaphysical basis is more complex. Although one could expect the dynamism of the idea of metempsychosis to be commensurate with the length of the series of successive transformations, it turns out that transmigration has come perilously close to the shapeshifting of fairy-tale contests, the bird image is very like a metaphor for lovers and a symbol for saved souls, and the function of the shrine resembles that of miracle-working saints who have received their reward for martyrdom and are in a position to administer divine justice. The metempsychotic framework seems more authentic in the versions with fewer transformations that stop short of the shrine phase. But regardless of the number of transformations, the idea of metempsychosis has often been obscured, either by various rational insertions or by lyric stylizations of the plant and bird phases.

The typical Spanish versions of the transformation motif examined in this study can be arranged as shown in the accompanying figure (p. 146). The versions A, B, and C, to the left of the dividing line, have no Christian terminology (the healing power in C is that of a spring and a river, effective for lovesickness). Version D, to the immediate right of the line, contains three successive transformations, which culminate in the shrine and spring with healing powers. Farther to the right are versions that lack one or more of the elements of D, but use Christian terminology and end with healing powers vested in the shrine or its substitute.

In D, E, F, G, H, and I, the healing powers, usually wielded by the chapel, but sometimes by a spring alone or even a plant, are clearly the most important element. F, G, H, I, and probably also E, can be considered syncopated variants of the three-stage version D, and of later date

TRANSFORMATIONS IN *CONDE OLINOS* BALLADS

	A	B	C	D	E	F	G	H	I
Plant(s)	•	•	•	•	•	•	•		
Birds		•		•	•				
Shrine				•	•	•			•
Spring (+ river in C)			•	•				•	
Healing powers	•			•	•	•	•	•	•

Examples: A—Catalán, pp. 209, 211. B—Bénichou, *Romancero,* p. 123. C—Menéndez y Pelayo, 10:73, 74-75. D—Cossío and Maza, nos. 36, 45. E—Cossío and Maza, nos. 37, 38, 46. F—Schindler, texts, p. 55. G—Larrea, 1:180. H—Cossío and Maza, nos. 42-44. I—Catalán, p. 218.

than D. The problem of the chronology of the versions on the left side and of their relationship to those on the right is more complicated.

If we try to match the different versions of *Conde Olinos* against the *romances* published during the first half of the sixteenth century and against those in the modern tradition, we might find that the shorter versions resemble more closely the former and the shrine version the latter. Type A, and particularly type B, of *Conde Olinos* would fit well among the brief, largely lyric, ballads that belong to the *Romancero viejo— Infante Arnaldos, Mora Moraima, Prisionero, Rosa fresca,* and others. The modern tradition, on the other hand, prefers a "good story" to "good taste." Some of its topics (incest, infanticide, fratricide, carnality of the clergy) might be deemed more suitable for a scandal sheet than for a collection of poetry; the endings are apt to distribute just rewards and punishments. The shrine version of *Conde Olinos* shows considerable affinity to this group. However, some other aspects of the problem need to be considered before a likely chronology can be decided upon.

There are several indications that versions of the transformation motif ending with the plant, bird, or shrine phase have coexisted for a long time and in the same places. For example, a mixed *romance—Conde Olinos* with an interpolation of *La enamorada de un muerto*—has endings of all three types. That the shrine version and the ending with the regrowth of grave-plants were known simultaneously, is evident in Cossío and Maza, no. 41: the olive trees are cut down and sprout again *after* they refuse to cure the queen. Also the Sephardic tradition in Morocco retains the miracle-revenge, the bird ending, and perhaps the plant ending (if this is the origin of the closing lines of *El pájaro verde,* quoted earlier). Hence one cannot classify the shrine version as a recent development, particularly since it has had time to be syncopated in many ways and to become established in the Azores with a final note of affection and gentle admonition, which makes it different from the Spanish versions in both word and spirit.

The resemblance to the *romances* published during the Renaissance may well be a valid criterion for dating the shorter versions of *Conde Olinos,* but this would not necessarily make them the earliest. Several of the lyric *romances* in the *Romancero viejo* are known to be truncated versions of earlier narrative ballads. As Ramón Menéndez Pidal has shown, *Infante Arnaldos,* with its suggestive ending, is the result of a series of systematic attempts to prune an adventure story. The printed *Romanceros* of the sixteenth century represent the taste of learned poets, collectors, and editors, who, in cultivating the traditional ballad, were guided by the refinement of their period. As in the case of *Arnaldos,* longer versions of *romances* may have existed before the sixteenth century, the earliest published version being one already revised, or at least selected, by a cultured hand.

Thus, a hypothesis that *Conde Olinos* lost its ending through the intervention of a Renaissance poet would appear more plausible than the assumption of Entwistle ("Second Thoughts," p. 17) that the ballad was "abbreviated by singers who forgot the last transformation or who could attach no meaning to the series." The syncopated shrine versions show that the final justice has been considerably more meaningful than the transformation of dead people into flora and fauna: the miraculous healing powers and the rebuke of the queen have proved to be the hardiest portion of the shrine version, while any or all of the intermediate steps have been dispensable.[12]

Yet, the real stumbling block is not so much the reason for a supposed abbreviation as the unlikelihood of any abbreviation that would ultimately result in a single transformation into plants. The long versions have no close parallel in European balladry, while the short version that ends with intertwining plants coincides, in both fact and feeling, with the ubiquitous rose-briar motif. Must we believe that by means of an amputation of the last ten or twenty lines (those that deal with transformations subsequent to the plant phase and lead to a moralistic conclusion), an anomalous ballad could be made to conform to an international type (rose-briar)? More than that: after the presumable shortening process reduced the multiple transformations to the emergence of grave-plants and their destruction, the adding of two octosyllabic lines (about the regrowth of the plants, as in Catalán, pp. 209 and 211) must have then produced a duplicate of the ending of *Tristan and Isolt,* the putative parent of the rose-briar commonplace in European balladry. Though not impossible, this kind of fortuitous assimilation would be most unusual.

As far as the popular meaning of the conclusion of *Conde Olinos* is concerned, the foregoing analysis persuades me to distinguish the *romance* from its early precursors. The transformation motif in the *Romancero* is generally regarded as a foreign import, and it is doubtful whether the concept of metempsychosis was ever an essential factor in the cultivation of *Conde Olinos* in Spain. The transformations could have rapidly attracted the more familiar and more convincing contest motif and final justice from fairy tales and the conventional form of a Christian miracle from legends or other ballads. Besides supplying a stronger, more definitive ending, the successive transformations with the binary rhythm of offense-defense must have been especially congenial to the Spanish *Romancero*, where series of antithetical verses are a traditional feature. All the while, the shorter versions also remained in the oral tradition, but became stylized under its abbreviating influence—the same influence that syncopated the shrine version. The different versions of the transformation motif obviously have continued to coexist, suffering a similar degeneration of the metempsychotic base and occasionally contaminating each other.

Conde Olinos is one of the most impressive examples of a ballad needing to be examined by various methods. Far from replacing the research of genealogy and the ordering of versions and variants by a scientific method, a contextual interpretation of symbols can begin only after such spadework has been done. While the purpose of contextual interpretation is to discover meanings beyond the directly obvious or the archaeologically ascertainable, the results of the probing may at times throw light on other kinds of problems. In the case of *Conde Olinos,* the changes in the function of the motifs suggested some reasons for its longevity. Whether a popular ballad lives or dies depends not so much on the quality of its ancestors as on its ability to evoke new associations that touch the values and concerns of successive generations. Those who would use the word "traditional" to denote something that has not kept up with the times fail to recognize that tradition—at least popular tradition—sustains only what is alive.

NOTES

Chapter 1

1. See, for example, "Folksong and Folksong Scholarship: Changing Approaches and Attitudes," in *A Good Tale and a Bonnie Tune,* ed. Mody C. Boatright et al. (Dallas, Tex., 1964), pp. 199-268, particularly the contributions of Tristram Coffin, John Greenway, and W. Edson Richmond.

2. The *romances* included by F. J. Wolf and C. Hofmann in *Primavera y flor de romances* (reissued by Marcelino Menéndez y Pelayo in *Antología de poetas líricos castellanos,* vols. 8 and 9) will be identified in the text by the abbreviation *Prim.* followed by the numbers assigned by Wolf and Hofmann.

3. See Ruth House Webber, *Formulistic Diction in the Spanish Ballad,* where classification of *romances* by earlier scholars is tabulated together with Webber's own findings.

Chapter 2

1. Arcadio de Larrea Palacín, *Romances de Tetuán,* 1:161. See also ibid., p. 164; *La flor de la marañuela,* ed. Diego Catalán et al., 2:12 ff.; José María de Cossío and Tomás Maza Solano, *Romancero popular de la Montaña,* 1:353 ff.

2. In the German equivalent, *Deutsche Volkslieder mit ihren Melodien,* ed. John Meier et al., 4:7, the brother is introduced as a lord, a knight, or alternatively a hunter: "Es ritt ein Jäger wohl über den Rhein."

3. *Danmarks gamle Folkeviser,* ed. Svend Grundtvig et al. (subsequent references as DgF), no. 436. English translation by R. C. A. Prior, *Ancient Danish Ballads.* See also DgF 475.

4. In the present study "Child ballads" will be cited by number. See Francis James Child, *The English and Scottish Popular Ballads.*

5. Marcelino Menéndez y Pelayo, *Antología de poetas líricos castellanos,* 9:193. But the hunt was just one of many occasions for a conversation between a king and his nobles. Two sixteenth-century versions of *Conde Claros* differ: "A caza va el emperador" (*Prim.* 191); "A misa va el emperador" (*Prim.* 192). The king simply goes out in Sephardic versions (Larrea, 1:92 ff.; Ramón Menéndez Pidal, "Romancero judío-español," no. 23).

6. Prior, 1:231. "Hawks" and "falcons" will be used loosely to designate various hunting birds. In the *Romancero* it is obvious that several species are mentioned interchangeably to fit rhythm and assonance.

7. *Prim.* 109; see also *Prim.* 171.

8. Dragutin Subotić, *Yugoslav Popular Ballads,* pp. 119-20.

9. John Bowring, *Servian Popular Poetry,* pp. 58-63.

10. Jonas Balys, *Lithuanian Narrative Folksongs,* p. 75; see also p. 135.

11. Ramón Menéndez Pidal, *Romancero hispánico,* 1:277.

12. Ibid.; see also Cossío and Maza, 1:88, 93.

13. *La flor de la marañuela,* 2:8. See discussion, José Pérez Vidal, "Romancero tradicional canario," *Revista de dialectología y tradiciones populares,* 7:278.

14. Julio Vicuña Cifuentes, *Romances populares y vulgares,* pp. 79-87.

15. *La flor de la marañuela,* 2:8; Menéndez y Pelayo, 10:181; Kurt Schindler, *Folk Music and Poetry of Spain and Portugal,* texts, pp. 58-59.

16. In an exceptional case such as the Sephardic variant recorded in Paul Bénichou, *Romancero judeo-español de Marruecos,* p. 142, the hunt is replaced by war and the curse limited to death by Moorish hand:

> Mi marido está en las guerras,   en las guerras de León,
> y para que más no volva   le echaré una baldición,
> que allí le maten los moros,   le saquen el coraçón.

17. Schindler, texts, p. 59; Theophilo Braga, *Cantos populares do Archipelago Açoriano,* p. 236; Manuel Milá y Fontanals, *Romancerillo catalán,* pp. 242 ff.

18. Costantino Nigra, *Canti popolari del Piemonte,* pp. 3 ff., 216 ff.

19. Braga, *Açoriano,* p. 376; see also p. 378.

20. *Prim.* 131: "Cuando el moro se iba a caza   quitábame la cadena." The Moor goes hunting also in a modern variant from Santander (Cossío and Maza, 1:379), a Sephardic text (Larrea, 1:170), and a Portuguese version (Theophilo Braga, *Romanceiro geral,* p. 114). A Sephardic variant (Larrea, 1:172) makes the usual change to "cuando el amo íbase de casa."

21. Menéndez y Pelayo, 10:95; see also 10:313; Cossío and Maza, 1:241 ff.

22. Menéndez y Pelayo, 10:94. Subsequently the mother-in-law slanders the wife to the husband and causes her death. See also Cossío and Maza, 1:241, and Braga, *Romanceiro geral,* p. 42.

23. Cossío and Maza, 1:46, and three other variants. This *romance* will be discussed further in connection with the introductory motif of the ominous hunt. The motif is lacking in the two versions from Asturias, Menéndez y Pelayo, 10:76-79.

24. Reinhold Trautmann, *Die Volksdichtung der Großrussen,* pp. 316, 269.

25. Sophie Jewett, *Folk-Ballads of Southern Europe,* p. 30.

26. Nigra, p. 247; George Doncieux, *Le Romancéro populaire de la France,* p. 127.

27. Cossío and Maza, 1:364; Menéndez y Pelayo, 10:217; see also 10:63.

28. "El mal cazador," p. 486.

29. Cf. *La esposa infiel,* above, where the curse invokes the hunter's death by Moorish lance and thus implies a human encounter.

30. Braga, *Romanceiro geral,* p. 39; *Açoriano,* p. 224.

31. Théodore Hersart de La Villemarqué, *Barzaz-Breiz,* p. 27.

32. *Deutsche Volkslieder,* 2:72; 4:321, 322, 324.

33. Julien Tiersot, *Chansons populaires recueillies dans les Alpes françaises,* p. 359.

34. Friedrich Karl von Erlach, *Die Volkslieder der Deutschen,* 2:109.
35. Cf. Trautmann, pp. 326, 332, 394 (in each, a raven instructs the hero).
36. Harriet M. Pawlowska, *Merrily We Sing,* p. 100; see also a Lithuanian version, Balys, p. 137.
37. The rural "asking of the bride" in many countries refers to her as some animal or bird.
38. John Meier, *Balladen,* 2:242. An extensive discussion of the love-hunt follows the versions of *Der Nachtjäger* (*Deutsche Volkslieder* 6:161-88) published after my study was completed. The motif of the wounded deer in Renaissance poetry—a confluence of biblical, classical, medieval, and popular currents—is discussed in María Rosa Lida, "Transmisión y recreación de temas grecolatinos en la poesía lírica española," *Revista de filología hispánica* 1 (1939), esp. "El ciervo herido y la fuente," pp. 31-52.
39. Some German songs (Erlach, 2:109; 3:115; 4:250) develop the encounter in the wood into a ridicule of the man within the milieu of a hunt; the hunter takes the girl to his cabin, but sleeps all night and is mocked by the girl in the morning; she either accepts or scorns his subsequent proposal of marriage.
40. *Romancero tradicional de las lenguas hispánicas,* ed. Ramón Menéndez Pidal et al., 2:151.
41. Cf. the polite greeting by the killer in *Frau von Weißenburg* (*Deutsche Volkslieder,* 1:301 ff.).
42. *Romancero tradicional,* 2:150; see also *Prim.* 26.
43. Menéndez Pidal, *Romancero hispánico,* 1:229-30; *Romancero tradicional,* 2:153.
44. Oluf, on his way to his bride, is caught in the forest by a dancing dwarf-maid, who offers him a great many gifts if he will live with her; his refusal brings him death.
45. Doncieux, p. 122. Cf. Nigra, pp. 164, 166 (variants D, F, G).
46. Nigra, p. 165. However, in a fairy tale (ibid., p. 169), a hunter finds a splendidly dressed woman—a fairy—who wants to marry him and punishes him for his refusal by giving him a box that contains a belt that flares up and kills him.
47. Menéndez Pidal, "Romancero judío-español," no. 75; also Bénichou, *Romancero,* p. 187.
48. C. Cabal, "Los temas maravillosos," p. 190.
49. Ramón Menéndez Pidal, *Flor nueva de romances viejos,* p. 195. Menéndez Pidal places this version in the late seventeenth century. In a few French variants, also, the hero meets Death in person. In a Venetian version (Jewett, p. 90), he is bitten by a *can barbin.*
50. The line, "Caía la nieve a copos   y el agua menuda y fría," has an isolated counterpart in the capture of Tam Lin (Child 39) by the Queen of Fairies on "a cauld day and a snell."
51. In some later versions, believed to be contaminated by *Graf Friedrich,* the Palatine discovers on the wedding night that his bride is dead; in some texts he too dies. On the relationship between *Rico Franco* and *Bluthochzeit,* see my article, "A New Genealogy for 'Rico Franco.' " An excellent compendium of examples and discussion of various hunt motifs is the chapter on *Rico Franco* in Samuel G. Armis-

tead and Joseph H. Silverman, *The Judeo-Spanish Ballad Chapbooks of Yacob Abraham Yoná*, pp. 241-54.

52. La Villemarqué, p. 26. Cf. a popular tradition cited by Scott (Child, 1:322) about the hart and hind that give Thomas the Rhymer the signal to return to the elf-queen.

53. "The Hunt and Prophecy Episode of the Poema de Fernán González" and "El misterioso origen de Fernán González." José de Onís adds to this genre a unicorn with a flaming horn; see "El celo de los duendes."

54. Theodor Kind, *Anthologie neugriechischer Volkslieder*, pp. 62-63.

55. Cf. a Slovenian ballad, *Deutsche Volkslieder*, 4:232.

56. Julio Caro Baroja, *Algunos mitos españoles y otros ensayos*, pp. 73-83. The Catalonian *mal cassador* belongs to the same group.

57. *Prim.* 147. Cf. the feats and fatal hunt of Lemminkäinen in the *Kalevala*.

58. Cf. *Willie and Earl Richard's Daughter* (Child 102).

59. Larrea, 2:54-55. Ferrets have been substituted for falcons on the Canary Islands (*La flor de la marañuela*, 2:7) and the Azores (Braga, *Açoriano*, p. 188).

60. The otherwise appropriate diagnosis of infantile mother fixation lies outside the scope of this study.

61. Caro Baroja, *Algunos mitos*, p. 54. Other nonhuman women, also, are recognizable by some irregularity; see the legends "La dama pie de cabra" and "La mujer marina," Menéndez y Pelayo, 12:52-54. Nevertheless, the hunters who found the goat-footed lady and the siren were eager to marry them.

62. Kathleen Hoagland, *1000 Years of Irish Poetry*, p. 66.

63. DgF 70. The linden tree with golden leaves that shelters the lady's bower bends down to earth when Young Svendal makes his entrance—a setting vaguely similar to that of *La infantina*. See also Armistead and Silverman, *Judeo-Spanish Ballad Chapbooks*, pp. 156-58.

64. The fusion of the two *romances* dates back to the sixteenth century: *Prim.* 154a. See also Menéndez y Pelayo, 10:89, and Cossío and Maza, 1:119. Many Portuguese versions add the ending of a third *romance, Don Bueso,* with the recognition between brother and sister, but tend to retain the motif of enchantment by seven fairies (Braga, *Romanceiro geral*, pp. 26, 28; idem, *Açoriano*, pp. 183, 185, 188).

65. Menéndez y Pelayo, 10:90 (cf. "donde canta la culebra, donde la culebra canta," p. 80; ". . . una fuente fría,/dó culebras cantan," p. 58).

66. Milá, p. 175. This lady also is combing her hair, but her beauty is elaborated by a description of her splendid clothing.

67. Cossío and Maza, 1:472; see also Schindler, texts, p. 83. Devoto (p. 484) believes that Christ is pictured here as a hunter of souls.

68. Cossío and Maza, 2:210. Some German contrafacta also have transformed the introductory hunt into a religious motif: "Es wolt ein jäger jagen, wolt jagen vor jenem holz" became "Es wolt gut Jäger jagen, wolt jagen im Himmelsthron" (Meier, *Balladen,* 1:23).

69. Ciro Bayo, *Romancerillo del Plata*, p. 51.

70. *Cancionero popular de la Provincia de Madrid,* coll. Manuel García Matos, ed. Marius Schneider and José Romeu Figueras, 1:45.

71. Julio Caro Baroja, "¿Es de origen mítico la 'leyenda' de la Serrana de la Vera?" p. 572.

72. Walter Morris Hart, *Ballad and Epic,* p. 29.

Chapter 3

1. Alfonso X el Sabio devoted a book to chess, another to the game of tables.

2. Urban Tigner Holmes, Jr., *Daily Living in the Twelfth Century,* p. 195.

3. *Prim.* 25. The account of the wedding of doña Lambla (= Lambra) in *Primera crónica general,* cited in *Romancero tradicional,* 2:108 ("Dio en somo de las tablas un grant golpe quel oyeron dentro en la villa") refers obviously to the tournament game.

4. Menéndez Pidal, "Romancero judío-español," no. 59; "Los romances tradicionales en América," pp. 17-21; *Romancero hispánico,* 2:352-53.

5. See also Braga, *Romanceiro geral,* p. 94, and J. B. de Almeida Garrett, *Romanceiro,* 2:291. Prior (3:143) quotes a story about Saint Louis, who, in returning from Egypt, "saw his brother, the Duke of Anjou, playing at tables on board the ship, and was so provoked at such levity that he seized the dice and the board, and threw them into the sea, and the money into the bargain."

6. François-Marie Luzel, *Gwerziou Breiz-Izel,* 1:240.

7. Cossío and Maza, 1:376; see also p. 374. In a German ballad (*Deutsche Volkslieder,* 1:233 ff.) a man gambles away his youngest son in an unspecified game.

8. Aurelio M. Espinosa, *Cuentos populares españoles,* 1:258; see also 1:274, and discussion, 2:473.

9. Nigra, pp. 451-52. Cf. Holmes, p. 195, and DgF 238.

10. Samuel G. Armistead and Joseph H. Silverman, "Hispanic Balladry among the Sephardic Jews of the West Coast," p. 237. "However," the authors add, "in some modern Castilian variants, as in the Sephardic text, the girl is wagered."

11. Menéndez Pidal, "Romancero judío-español," no. 112. Being wagered in a chess game is not restricted to mortal wives; it happened also to Etain, the Irish goddess (Hoagland, p. 74).

12. Nigra, p. 199; see also Tiersot, p. 135.

13. *Prim.* 121. In the Sephardic versions from Tetuan (Larrea, 1:199 ff.), Xulianesa and the Moor are playing with dice.

14. Luis Santullano, *Romancero español,* p. 965.

15. Isabel Florence Hapgood, *The Epic Songs of Russia,* p. 200.

16. *Prim.* 173; see also Braga, *Romanceiro geral,* p. 94; Almeida Garrett, 2:291.

17. *Romancero hispánico,* 2:175; see also Menéndez y Pelayo, 12:202.

Chapter 4

1. Cf. *El sacrificio de Isaac,* in Diego Catalán, *Por campos del romancero,* pp. 56-58.

2. *Romancero tradicional,* 5:149-90 (many variants).

3. Larrea, 2:115. The color of clothing is often omitted in the *Romancero* even

in detailed descriptions, such as that of the Queen of Heaven (Cossío and Maza, 2:142), as she passes in worldly opulence through town: "Con zapatito picado y media de fina seda,/y una toca toledana,   ¡válgame Dios qué hermosa era!"

4. P. Eisner, *Volkslieder der Slaven,* p. 87.

5. Luzel, 2:528; *Deutsche Volkslieder,* 4:39, 2; Balys, p. 56; Nigra, p. 344; Joseph Canteloube, *Anthologie des chants populaires français,* 2:192; Trautmann, p. 162; *Deutsche Volkslieder,* 2:69, 70.

6. Menéndez y Pelayo, 10:146; Cossío and Maza, 1:59; Braga, *Romanceiro geral,* p. 52; Child 155 A.

7. DgF 47, 48, 145, 259; Balys, p. 51. Cf. Child, 5:284; DgF 265.

8. Menéndez y Pelayo, 10:193. After this, she offers other creature comforts: white bread, mattresses, a carriage, a fountain.

9. DgF 263, trans. Prior, 3:90.

10. Cossío and Maza, 2:134; Vicuña, p. 133.

11. DgF 353, trans. E. M. Smith-Dampier, *A Book of Danish Ballads,* ed. Axel Olrik, p. 206.

12. *The Kalevala,* comp. Elias Lönnrot, trans. Francis Peabody Magoun, Jr., poem 4.

13. *Lord Thomas and Fair Annet* (Child 73); *Herr Peders Slegfred* (DgF 210); *Tristes noces,* Doncieux, p. 340; *Danze e funerali,* Nigra, p. 159; *Bodas,* Milá, p. 257. See also Matthew J. C. Hodgart, *The Ballads,* pp. 90-91; Marta Pohl, *Gemeinsame Themen englisch-schottischer und französischer Volksballaden,* passim.

14. W. J. Entwistle, "La dama de Aragón"; Samuel G. Armistead and Joseph H. Silverman, "La dama de Aragón"; idem, *Judeo-Spanish Ballad Chapbooks,* pp. 322-31.

15. Larrea (2:122) notes that *La bella en misa* is always sung before the Sephardic *Verjicos (Virgilios),* where a lady's mourning for the imprisoned Verjicos brings about his release. In both the Sephardic and the modern peninsular *Capitán burlado* (Bénichou, *Romancero,* p. 265; Cossío and Maza, 2:25), verses reminiscent of *La bella en misa* describe a girl who is seen at Mass and subsequently pursued by a lecherous captain, but evades him successfully by exchanging clothes with a servant.

16. Arthur León Campa, *Spanish Folk-Poetry in New Mexico,* p. 75. See also my "*Sofía mía* en el contexto europeo."

17. Menéndez y Pelayo, 10:100; Nigra, p. 119; Doncieux, p. 445.

18. Armistead and Silverman, "La dama de Aragón," p. 235, quoting B. Gil, *Romances populares de Extremadura recogidos de la tradición oral* (Badajoz, 1944), p. 90.

19. Cossío and Maza, 1:182 ff.; Doncieux, p. 199.

20. Child 48; *Deutsche Volkslieder,* 2:72 ff.

21. Milá, p. 161; in *L'Escrivette,* Doncieux, pp. 131-32, the regretted finery includes silk, satin, and shoes of morocco leather.

22. Menéndez y Pelayo, 10:78; see also p. 77 (only mourning clothes); Cossío and Maza, 1:45 (complete antithesis), and 1:46-47 (only festive clothes). See also Armistead and Silverman, *Judeo-Spanish Ballad Chapbooks,* p. 176. The alleged ardor

and eroticism in the departure, as expressed by clothes, has parallels in the Dutch and German Halewijn-Ulinger ballads.

23. Menéndez y Pelayo, 10:84; Larrea, 1:70; Menéndez y Pelayo, 10:48; Larrea, 1:142; *Prim.* 92a.

24. Menéndez Pidal (*Flor nueva*, pp. 197-98) refers to it as a seventeenth-century version.

25. La Villemarqué, p. 28; Nigra, p. 162.

26. Julio Caro Baroja (*Ensayo sobre la literatura de cordel*, p. 411) relates the illustrations found on broadsides to medieval and Renaissance art forms: "El procedimiento de cuadricular una superficie, para dibujar o grabar algo en cada cuadrícula, de suerte que en el conjunto se desarrolle un tema, es viejísimo. Pero sin ir a tiempos demasiado remotos, lo podemos hallar aplicado en los retablos medievales y renacentistas, con las vidas de santos, sus milagros, etc.; desarrollados de modo cronológico y en forma decorativa menos sistemática, también se empleó en los azulejos que en Valencia y Cataluña tienen una evidente correspondencia formal con las aleluyas."

Chapter 5

1. Cossío and Maza, 2:8 ff. See also Braga, *Romanceiro geral*, pp. 8, 12; idem, *Açoriano*, p. 212. Girls, while combing, are noticed by prospective grooms (Canteloube, 4:232; Kind, p. 152; Pawlowska, p. 57).

2. Schindler, texts, p. 106. See also Larrea, 2:273; Bayo, p. 36.

3. Théo Brandão, "La Condessa," p. 595. A Lithuanian wedding song (Balys, p. 115) begins by telling about a girl who sits on a chair in the whirlpool in the river Nemunas; she combs her hair and weeps bitterly since she has no family to assist at the wedding.

4. *Cancionero de romances impreso en Amberes sin año*, fol. 228.

5. Manuel Alvar, "Patología y terapéutica rapsódicas," pp. 28-29. Detailed enumerations of a woman's features, typical of Sephardic *romances*, frequently include hair; *La bella en misa* (Menéndez Pidal, "Romancero judío-español," no. 133); "Su cabeza una toronxa,   sus cabellos briles son"; variant from Salonika (Armistead and Silverman, "Hispanic Balladry," p. 238): "Kuando los tomó a peinare,   en ellos despuntó el sol."

6. La Villemarqué, p. liv. Cf. Gervasius of Tilbury, *Otia imperialia*, quoted by Menéndez y Pelayo, 10:115.

7. Menéndez y Pelayo, 10:90. Golden comb also: Cossío and Maza, 1:119; Braga, *Açoriano*, pp. 183, 185, 188; Milá, p. 175.

8. Larrea, 2:54-55. See also *Prim.* 151; Menéndez Pidal, "Romancero judío-español," no. 114. Her hair falls over her entire body in José Leite de Vasconcellos, "Dois romances peninsulares," p. 396.

9. Ramón Menéndez Pidal, *En torno al Poema del Cid*, p. 184; Caro Baroja, *Algunos mitos*, p. 62. The latter (pp. 47-53) also describes the *lamias* of the Basque country, who are said to go from house to house, looking for a comb; at other times they comb their hair with a beautiful golden comb, sitting on a rock in the river or in

front of their cave. Mari, an ancient Basque deity, was very fond of combing and used a golden comb.

10. Cossío and Maza, 2:140-41. See also ibid., pp. 238, 276; Braga, *Açoriano,* p. 354; Menéndez y Pelayo, 10:216. See ibid., 10:148, on the fusion of the person of the Virgin and old folk beliefs about the summer solstice.

11. "The Scottish Ballads," p. 243. Speirs's interpretation is rejected by Matthew J. C. Hodgart, *Ballads,* pp. 135-36.

12. Balys, p. 52; Tiersot, p. 118; Nigra, p. 418.

13. Santullano. p. 1092. See also Canteloube, 1:192; Milá, p. 179.

14. José Massot Muntaner, "El romancero tradicional español en Mallorca," p. 168.

15. David Elnecavé, "Folklore de los sefardíes de Turquía," p. 123.

16. María Rosa Lida, "El romance de la Misa de amor," p. 38, pinpoints the use of cosmetics in ballads as a sign of the light-minded woman.

17. Menéndez y Pelayo, 9:219; Menéndez Pidal, "Romancero judío-español," no. 82. A young wife regrets her marriage on her wedding day, as she is combing, in *Celinos y la adúltera* (Armistead and Silverman, *Judeo-Spanish Ballad Chapbooks,* p. 227).

18. Menéndez y Pelayo, 10:123. Black hair is very rare in the ballads of western Europe; in this *romance,* it may be taken as both an omen and a symbol of bad character.

19. Child 35, 36; DgF 89, 133; Nigra, p. 245; Menéndez y Pelayo, 10:66; Cossío and Maza, 1:103.

20. Larrea, 1:170-73; Bénichou, *Romancero,* p. 205; Braga, *Açoriano,* pp. 323, 325; Braga, *Romanceiro geral,* pp. 113-15. Bénichou, who in *Creación poética en el romancero tradicional* devotes a chapter to this *romance,* does not analyze the detail of lousing.

21. Bénichou, *Romancero,* p. 63. See also Larrea, 1:204, and *Mujer de Juan Lorenzo* (Larrea, 1:59). In a fairy tale from Seville (Espinosa, 1:337), a captive lady kills a giant with a magic egg, while lousing him. On the lighter side is a Russian ballad (Eisner, p. 65): when the boy awakes, gone is not only the girl who had combed his hair, but also his tent, his horse, his saddle—and his fair locks.

22. Ninon A. M. Leader, *Hungarian Classical Ballads and Their Folklore,* pp. 107, 301.

23. Although the *Romancero* contains such vows only as made by men, in Spanish history Isabel Clara Eugenia, daughter of Philip II, promised not to change her shirt until Ostend was conquered—an enterprise that took three years to complete (see Menéndez Pidal, *Romancero hispánico,* 1:268).

24. Archer Taylor ("Una comparación tentativa de temas de baladas inglesas y españolas," p. 20) notes the similarity of the vows in *Prim.* 165 and *Clerk Saunders,* but does not analyze the respective situations. Child (2:156) enumerates British and some foreign ballads that contain vows of austerity.

Chapter 6

1. William James Entwistle, "El Conde Olinos," p. 238; idem, "Second Thoughts Concerning El Conde Olinos," p. 14; Leo Spitzer, "The Folkloristic Pre-Stage of the Spanish Romance 'Conde Arnaldos,'" pp. 173-87. Bénichou (*Romancero*, pp. 212, 335-36) discredits the hypotheses of Entwistle and Spitzer. See also the thoughtful analysis of *Conde Olinos* by Armistead and Silverman, *Judeo-Spanish Ballad Chapbooks*, pp. 152-73.

2. Gordon Hall Gerould, *The Ballad of Tradition*, pp. 144-45.

3. See also Daniel Devoto, "Un no aprehendido canto," in *Ábaco*, vol. 1 (Madrid, 1969), pp. 22-44.

4. Canteloube, 1:157; 2:381; 3:118, 197, 223; 4:62, 115, 306, 326; Doncieux, p. 445; Nigra, p. 119.

5. Friedrich von der Leyen, *Deutsche Dichtung des Mittelalters*, p. 271. Konrad Huber ("Romance del Conde Arnaldos"), attributes the similarities to a common pool of motifs, probably located in France.

6. Menéndez y Pelayo, 10:146; ibid, p. 139; *Prim.* 121; *Prim.* 124; *Prim.* 195; Larrea, 1:166; Milá, p. 236; *Prim.* 165 (see chap. 2).

7. Broadside version, Ramón Menéndez Pidal, "Poesía popular y poesía tradicional en la literatura española," p. 65. See also Bénichou, *Romancero*, p.207.

8. Portuguese *romances* that spell out the text of the song that wins the singer release from prison will be discussed later.

9. See Menéndez Pidal, "Poesía popular," pp. 68-69.

10. Some variants of *Conde Olinos* spell out his song as a prayer for protection of the horse, in some cases from sandbanks and high winds, obviously modeled after a protective song for a ship, such as that in *Infante Arnaldos*. See Menéndez y Pelayo, 10:72, 74; Braga, *Romanceiro geral*, p. 37.

11. Braga, *Açoriano*, pp. 258-59. In the German *Schloß in Österreich*, the young prisoner objects to his mother's request in almost the same words as Dom Pedro; he remains firm in his refusal and is executed (*Deutsche Volkslieder*, 1:257).

12. Catalán, *Por campos del romancero*, p. 244. This *romance* does not contain a text of the song that the boy sings. See also Menéndez y Pelayo, 10:308.

13. Milá, p. 165; in variant C, his song is taken for a proof of innocence: "Que si ell culpa tenía   no cantaría aixi, nó"; Jewett, p. 168; Nigra, p. 332.

14. See chaps. 3, 4. Note also the devout nuance in the first-person song, which in a version of *Conde Niño* from the Canary Islands precedes the magic effect on man and nature: "Mentres mi caballo baña,   quiero cantar un cantar,/ni muy alto ni muy bajo,   qu'al cielo deba llegar" (*La flor de la marañuela*, 2:47).

15. Cossío and Maza, 1:138; see also pp. 77, 78. On the other hand, Gerineldo's name appears in some variants of *Conde Olinos*.

16. Schindler, texts, p. 60; also p. 59, and many Canarian, Sephardic, Portuguese, and Catalan versions.

17. Nigra, p. 129; Luzel, 1:170; DgF 465, 220, 39; Kind, p. 94; Bénichou, *Romancero*, p. 149, and Larrea, 1:322; DgF 65.

18. *Digenes Akrites*, ed. and trans. John Mavrogordato, p. 89; Hapgood, p. 180.

19. Ramón Menéndez Pidal uses "que por mí quiere finar" in his hybrid version, *Flor nueva,* p. 117.

20. *Romancero tradicional,* 3:24-45; see also Armistead and Silverman, *Judeo-Spanish Ballad Chapbooks,* p. 301, n. 11; DgF 72; *Deutsche Volkslieder,* 3:267; Luzel, 2:424.

21. Cossío and Maza, 1:185; see also Milá, pp. 202 ff.; Doncieux, p. 200; Kind, p. 133; Luzel, 1:198; Nigra, p. 371; La Villemarqué, p. 147.

22. Menéndez y Pelayo, 10:78; see also Armistead and Silverman, *Judeo-Spanish Ballad Chapbooks,* pp. 176-77.

23. Larrea, 2:188; see also Menéndez y Pelayo, 10:149-50. Cf. *Young Beichan* (Child 53 H).

24. Child (2:511-12) quotes from O'Curry, *On the Manners and Customs of the Ancient Irish,* 3 vols. (London, 1873) 3:214, the three feats that give distinction to a harper—performed by Daghda, the Druid, in the hall of his enemies: he made the women cry tears, the women and youth burst into laughter, and the entire host fall asleep. Hapgood (p. 46, n.) remarks that falling asleep was regarded among the ancient Slavs as the highest compliment that could be paid to a musician.

25. Hapgood, pp. 217-19; see also Trautmann, p. 246.

26. Maud Karpeles, *Folk Songs from Newfoundland,* 1:31.

27. Menéndez Pidal, "Romancero judío-español," no. 142. See also Santullano, pp. 1026-27; Armistead and Silverman, *Judeo-Spanish Ballad Chapbooks,* pp. 352 ff.

Chapter 7

1. For the sake of clarity, the young man will be called Olinos throughout this discussion, although he appears also as Niño, Fernandito, Longinos, Olivos, Alimán, Doardos, Nilo, etc. For copious examples and highly perceptive analyses of *Conde Olinos,* see Armistead and Silverman, *Judeo-Spanish Ballad Chapbooks,* pp. 152-73, and Bénichou, *Romancero,* pp. 123-28, 334-38.

2. Pohl (p. 30) speculates that having an outside power, especially a priest, destroy the plants, may be an English way of combating superstition.

3. Since in this chapter many consecutive texts of *Conde Olinos* from Cossío and Maza are cited, the versions will be identified by numbers (35-46) rather than pages (1:75-87).

4. See La Villemarqué, p. 28. Similarly without destruction of the trees are the texts of *Don Luis de Montalbán* (Catalan versions of *Vuelta del navegante,* in *Romancero tradicional,* 3:24-43) which end with a two-stage transformation. For repeated transformations see Hapgood, pp. 37-38 (two rivers, two cypresses, no destruction), and Subotić, pp. 6-7 (a stepmother poisons two boys and destroys them in two successive stages as basil plants and pines).

5. Onís, "Celo de los duendes," pp. 223-24. Cf. a New World mutation of *Barbara Allen,* in *Colorado Folksong Bulletin* 1, no. 3 (1962):4, where Sweet William requests:

> Go dig my grave, go dig it deep
> Place a marble stone at my head and feet,

And on my breast place a snow-white dove,
To prove to the world that I died for love.

6. Cossío and Maza, nos. 35-38, 40, 45, 46; Braga, *Romanceiro geral,* p. 38.

7. Since *paloma* and *gavilán* appear in this manner only in direct speech or first-person narrative (as do hawk and dove also in Polish, Russian, and Yugoslav ballads), I cannot concur with Entwistle ("Second Thoughts," p. 13) in assuming that the dove who comes to rescue Olinos in a version from Asturias is in the fact the princess in her own, human shape. In the latter case, also, the explanation she gives of her identity to Olinos ("soy la infanta, conde Olinos") would be superfluous.

8. In Sephardic *romances,* the symbolism of birds seems ambiguous: a white dove and a green bird are used interchangeably for victim or villain in *La infanticida* and *El pájaro verde;* in neither ballad is there any mention of death before the metamorphosis.

9. A parallel exists in Hungarian ballads: the grave-plants or birds cast an elaborate curse on the guilty mother, using in some cases Christian terminology: "For you are damned, but I have found salvation," or "May there be no blessing on you from Heaven" (Leader, pp. 192, 129).

10. Much more loosely, *Conde Olinos* can be linked to a large body of European folksongs, the "Metamorphoses" (or "Transformations"; mentioned, for instance, by Child in connection with *The Twa Magicians*). The "Metamorphoses" consist of a hypothetical contest between a girl and an impatient suitor, each proposing a new shape to best the previous one, until the girl gives in. Despite the similarity of a few component parts, the relationship between the "Metamorphoses" and *Conde Olinos* is not likely to go beyond common inspiration in fairy tales.

11. For gruesome humor, see Sephardic versions in which the birds are killed and eaten; their bones, thrown into the sea, turn into fish; the queen eats the fish and buries their bones, but they change into a snake and a scorpion and settle on the queen's neck (Armistead and Silverman, *Judeo-Spanish Ballad Chapbooks,* p. 166; Bénichou, *Romancero,* pp. 125-26).

12. Bénichou (*Romancero,* pp. 335-36) also remains unconvinced by Entwistle, though for different reasons. Armistead and Silverman conclude that the vengeance variants "may well go back to some relatively archaic form of *El conde Olinos*" (*Judeo-Spanish Ballad Chapbooks,* p. 166).

BIBLIOGRAPHY

(Anonymous works and ballad collections with several
editors are listed by title rather than by editor.)

Almeida Garrett, J. B. de. *Romanceiro*. Revised by Fernando de Castro
Pires de Lima. 3 vols. Lisbon, 1963.

Alvar, Manuel. "Patología y terapéutica rapsódicas: Como una canción
se convierte en romance." *Revista de filología española* 42 (1958-59):
19-35.

Armistead, Samuel G., and Silverman, Joseph H. "La dama de Aragón:
Its Greek and Romance Congeners." *Kentucky Romance Quarterly* 14
(1967):227-38.

———. "Hispanic Balladry among the Sephardic Jews of the West
Coast." *Western Folklore* 19 (1960): 229-44.

———. *The Judeo-Spanish Ballad Chapbooks of Yacob Abraham Yoná*.
Folk Literature of the Sephardic Jews, 1. Berkeley, Cal., 1971.

Balys, Jonas. *Lithuanian Narrative Folksongs: A Description of Types
and a Bibliography*. Washington, D. C., 1954.

Bayo, Ciro. *Romancerillo del Plata*. Madrid, 1913.

Bénichou, Paul. *Creación poética en el romancero tradicional*. Madrid,
1968.

———. *Romancero judeo-español de Marruecos*. Madrid, 1968.

Bowring, John. *Servian Popular Poetry*. London, 1827.

Braga, Theophilo. *Cantos populares do Archipelago Açoriano*. Oporto,
1869.

———. *Romanceiro geral*. Coimbra, 1867.

Brandão, Théo. "La Condessa." *Revista de dialectología y tradiciones
populares* 10 (1954): 591-643.

Cabal, C. "Los temas maravillosos: La significación de una
palabra = Huerco." *Revista de dialectología y tradiciones populares* 2
(1946): 183-95.

Campa, Arthur Leon. *Spanish Folk-Poetry in New Mexico*. Albuquerque,
N. M., 1946.

Cancionero de romances impreso en Amberes sin año. New facsim. ed. by
Ramón Menéndez Pidal. Madrid, 1945.

Cancionero popular de la Provincia de Madrid. Collected by Manuel García Matos. Edited by Marius Schneider and José Romeu Figueras. 2 vols. Barcelona, 1951-52.

Canteloube, Joseph. *Anthologie des chants populaires français groupés et presentés par pays ou provinces.* 4 vols. Paris, 1951.

Caro Baroja, Julio. *Algunos mitos españoles y otros ensayos. 2d ed.* Madrid, 1944.

―――. *Ensayo sobre la literatura de cordel.* Madrid, 1969.

―――. "¿Es de origen mítico la 'leyenda' de la Serrana de la Vera?" *Revista de dialectología y tradiciones populares* 2 (1946): 569-72.

Catalán, Diego. *Por campos del romancero: Estudios sobre la tradición oral moderna.* Madrid, 1970.

Child, Francis James. *The English and Scottish Popular Ballads.* 5 vols. Boston, 1882-98.

Cossío, José María de, and Maza Solano, Tomás. *Romancero popular de la Montaña: Colección de romances tradicionales.* 2 vols. Santander, 1933-34.

Danmarks gamle Folkeviser. Edited by Svend Grundtvig et al. 11 vols. Copenhagen, 1853-1938.

Deutsche Volkslieder mit ihren Melodien: Balladen. Edited by John Meier et al. 6 vols. to date. Berlin and Freiburg, 1935-.

Devoto, Daniel. "El mal cazador." In *Studia philologica: Homenaje ofrecido a Dámaso Alonso,* vol. 1. Madrid, 1960.

Digenes Akrites. Edited and translated by John Mavrogordato. Oxford, 1956.

Doncieux, George. *Le Romancéro populaire de la France: Choix de chansons populaires françaises.* Paris, 1904.

Eisner, P. *Volkslieder der Slaven.* Leipzig, 1926.

Elnecavé, David. "Folklore de los sefardíes de Turquía." *Sefarad* 24 (1964):121-36.

Entwistle, William James. "El Conde Olinos." *Revista de filología española* 35 (1951):237-48.

―――. "La dama de Aragón." *Hispanic Review* 6 (1938): 185-92.

―――. "Second Thoughts Concerning *El Conde Olinos.*" *Romance Philology* 7 (1953): 10-18.

Erlach, Friedrich Karl von. *Die Volkslieder der Deutschen.* 5 vols. Mannheim, 1834.

Espinosa, Aurelio M. *Cuentos populares españoles*. 3 vols. Madrid, 1946.

La flor de la marañuela: Romancero general de las islas Canarias. Ed. Diego Catalán et al. 2 vols. Madrid, 1969.

Gerould, Gordon Hall. *The Ballad of Tradition*. New York, 1957.

Hapgood, Isabel Florence. *The Epic Songs of Russia*. London, 1915.

Hart, Walter Morris. *Ballad and Epic: A Study in the Development of Narrative Art*. Boston, 1907.

Hoagland, Kathleen. *1000 Years of Irish Poetry*. New York, 1953.

Hodgart, Matthew J. C. *The Ballads*. New York, 1962.

Holmes, Urban Tigner, Jr. *Daily Living in the Twelfth Century*. Madison, Wis., 1964.

Huber, Konrad. "Romance del Conde Arnaldos." *Vox romanica* 27 (1968): 138-60.

Jewett, Sophie. *Folk-Ballads of Southern Europe*. New York, 1913.

The Kalevala; or, Poems of the Kaleva District. Compiled by Elias Lönnrot. Translated by Francis Peabody Magoun, Jr. Cambridge, Mass., 1963.

Karpeles, Maud. *Folk Songs from Newfoundland*. London, [1934?].

Keller, J. P. "The Hunt and Prophecy Episode of the *Poema de Fernán González*." *Hispanic Review* 23 (1955): 251-58.

————. "El misterioso origen de Fernán González." *Nueva revista de filología hispánica* 10 (1956): 41-44.

Kind, Theodor. *Anthologie neugriechischer Volkslieder*. Leipzig, 1861.

Larrea Palacín, Arcadio de. *Romances de Tetuán*. 2 vols. Madrid, 1952.

La Villemarqué, Théodore Hersart de. *Barzaz-Breiz: Chants populaires de la Bretagne*. 6th ed. Paris, 1867.

Leader, Ninon A. M. *Hungarian Classical Ballads and Their Folklore*. Cambridge, England, 1967.

Leite de Vasconcellos, José. "Dois romances peninsulares." *Revista de filología española* 9 (1922):395-98.

Leyen, Friedrich von der. *Deutsche Dichtung des Mittelalters*. Frankfurt a.M., 1962.

Lida, María Rosa. "El romance de la Misa de amor." *Revista de filología hispánica* 3 (1941):24-42.

Luzel, François-Marie. *Gwerziou Breiz-Izel: Chants populaires de la Basse-Bretagne*. 2 vols. Lorient, 1868-74.

Massot Muntaner, José. "El romancero tradicional español en

Mallorca.'' *Revista de dialectología y tradiciones populares* 17 (1961): 157-73.

Meier, John. *Balladen.* 2 vols. Leipzig, 1935-36.

Menéndez y Pelayo, Marcelino. *Antología de poetas líricos castellanos.* 14 vols. Biblioteca Clásica. Madrid, 1890-1916.

Menéndez Pidal, Ramón. *En torno al Poema del Cid.* Barcelona, [1963].

————. *Flor nueva de romances viejos.* 13th ed. Buenos Aires, ''Austral,'' 1962.

————. ''Poesía popular y poesía tradicional en la literatura española.'' In his *Los romances de América y otros estudios.* 4th ed. Buenos Aires, 1945.

————. *Romancero hispánico.* 2 vols. Madrid, 1953.

————. ''Romancero judío-español.'' In his *Los romances de América y otros estudios.* 4th ed. Buenos Aires, 1945.

————. ''Los romances tradicionales en América.'' In his *Los romances de América y otros estudios.* 4th ed. Buenos Aires, 1945.

Milá y Fontanals, Manuel. *Romancerillo catalán: Canciones tradicionales.* 2d ed. Barcelona, 1882.

Nigra, Costantino. *Canti popolari del Piemonte.* Turin, 1888. Reprint. Turin, 1957.

Olrik, Axel. *A Book of Danish Ballads.* Translated by E. M. Smith-Dampier. Princeton, N. J., 1939.

Onís, José de. ''El celo de los duendes: Una variante americana del romance del *Conde Olinos.*'' *Cuadernos americanos* 23 (1964): 219-29.

Pawlowska, Harriet M. *Merrily We Sing: 105 Polish Folksongs.* Detroit, Mich., 1961.

Pérez Vidal, José. ''Romancero tradicional canario (Isla de la Palma).'' *Revista de dialectología y tradiciones populares* 5 (1949): 435-70; 6 (1950): 554-73; 7 (1951): 266-91, 424-45.

Pohl, Marta. *Gemeinsame Themen englisch-schottischer und französischer Volksballaden.* Beihefte zum Jahrbuch für Volksliedforschung, Heft 4. Berlin, 1940.

Primavera y flor de romances. Edited by F. J. Wolf and C. Hofmann. Berlin. 1856. Reissued by Marcelino Menéndez y Pelayo in *Antología de poetas líricos castellanos,* vols. 8 and 9.

Prior, Richard Chandler Alexander. *Ancient Danish Ballads.* 3 vols. London, 1860.

Rogers, Edith. "A New Genealogy for 'Rico Franco.' " *Journal of American Folklore* 82 (1969): 369-73.

———. "*Sofía mía* en el contexto europeo." *Revista de dialectología y tradiciones populares* 28 (1972): 275-81.

Romancero tradicional de las lenguas hispánicas (español-portugués-catalán-sefardí). Edited by Ramón Menéndez Pidal et al. 8 vols to date. Madrid, 1957-.

Santullano, Luis. *Romancero español.* Madrid, 1943.

Schindler, Kurt. *Folk Music and Poetry of Spain and Portugal (Música y poesía popular de España y Portugal).* New York, 1941.

Smith-Dampier, E. M., trans. See Olrik, Axel.

Speirs, John. "The Scottish Ballads." In *The Critics & the Ballad.* Edited by MacEdward Leach and Tristram P. Coffin. Carbondale, Ill., 1961.

Spitzer, Leo. "The Folkloristic Pre-Stage of the Spanish Romance 'Conde Arnaldos.' " *Hispanic Review* 23 (1955): 173-87.

Subotić, Dragutin. *Yugoslav Popular Ballads: Their Origin and Development.* Cambridge, England, 1932.

Taylor, Archer. "Una comparación tentativa de temas de baladas inglesas y españolas." *Folklore americano* 4, no. 4 (1956): 5-27.

Tiersot, Julien. *Chansons populaires recueillies dans les Alpes françaises (Savoie et Dauphiné).* Grenoble, 1903.

Trautmann, Reinhold. *Die Volksdichtung der Großrussen.* Vol. 1, *Das Heldenlied.* Heidelberg, 1935.

Vicuña Cifuentes, Julio. *Romances populares y vulgares.* Santiago, Chile, 1912.

Webber, Ruth House. *Formulistic Diction in the Spanish Ballad.* University of California Publications in Modern Philology, vol. 34, no. 2. Berkeley, 1951.

TITLE INDEX
(Ballads)

General Index